Copyright Photograph by The Dover St. Studios, Ltd.

MAJOR PROPHETS OF TO-DAY

MAJOR PROPHETS
OF TO-DAY

BY

EDWIN E. SLOSSON, M.S., Ph.D.

Essay Index Reprint Series

 BOOKS FOR LIBRARIES PRESS
FREEPORT, NEW YORK

First Published 1914
Reprinted 1968

LIBRARY OF CONGRESS CATALOG CARD NUMBER:
68-8493

PRINTED IN THE UNITED STATES OF AMERICA

TO MY WIFE

MAY PRESTON SLOSSON

WHO WAS THE COMPANION OF MY PILGRIMAGE

TO THE OLD WORLD

IN SEARCH OF NEW PROPHETS

THIS VOLUME

IS AFFECTIONATELY DEDICATED

PREFACE

EACH age has its own prophets, men who bring to it distinctive messages and present them in such effective form as to sway the currents of contemporary thought. No age perhaps has had more diverse theories of life and the meaning of things presented to it than our own, and certainly none has ever given such an opportunity for the original thinker to reach quickly a world-wide audience as he can now through the medium of cheap books and free schools.

This volume originated in my own desire to find out what was being said by certain persons who, I had reason to believe, were worth attention. But unless one is abnormally selfish, he always wants to introduce others to an interesting acquaintance. It is then simply as introductions that I would wish the following chapters to be taken. In one way or another such men are influencing the thought of all of us, but since we mostly get their philosophy at second hand — or at third, fourth, or nth hand — we fail to recognize its origin and are apt to misconceive its intent. Ideas that reach us in fragmentary form, and often after multiple translation through minds sometimes alien or hostile, are not very useful. It is always safer to drink at the source. I have endeavored to give some idea of the scope and character of each man's work, so that the reader may judge for himself whether it is profitable for him to follow up the acquaintance. If he does, he will find at the end of the chapter directions how to proceed further.

We imagine we can understand a man better if we can see his face, even his photograph. This may be a superstition, but, if so, it is a superstition worth deferring to by one who aspires to be an interpreter. So in the summer of 1910 I went to see the six men included in this first volume in their homes, not with the hope of getting any new and unpublished opinions, not with the expectation of gaining a personal acquaintance that would give me any deeper insight into their mental processes, but merely to convince myself that they are flesh and blood, instead of paper and ink. If I can convince the reader of this, my purpose will be accomplished.

In the choice of names to be included in the list, I was guided primarily by the idea that I should be most likely to interest others in the men who have most interested me. Since the object of the book is to serve as an introduction to the works of the authors, not as a substitute for them, the choice was limited to those who have given expression to their philosophical views in a sufficiently popular form to be attractive to the general reader. It was necessary to select representatives of diverse types of thought, and it was not possible to confine the choice to the philosophical profession, for in our day philosophy has escaped from its classroom and often displays more activity outside than in it. So I have included men of science and letters as well as philosophers of the chair.

The group comprised in this volume includes: Maurice Maeterlinck, dramatist and essayist, interpreter of the animate and inanimate world; Henri Bergson, of the Collège de France, whose intuitive philosophy has been introduced into America by the late William James; Henri Poincaré, of the French Academy, mathematician and astronomer; Elie Metchnikoff, director of the Pasteur Institute in Paris, author of studies in optimistic philosophy; Wilhelm Ostwald, of Leipzig University, recipient of the Nobel prize for chemistry in 1909, founder of the *Annals of Natural Philos-*

PREFACE

ophy, and Ernst Haeckel, of Jena University, veteran zoölogist, champion of Darwinism and Monism, author of the "Riddle of the Universe."

In large part the chapters of this volume have appeared in the *Independent* during the last three years in a series under the general title of "Twelve Major Prophets of To-day", which includes similar articles on Rudolf Eucken, Bernard Shaw, H. G. Wells, G. K. Chesterton, F. C. S. Schiller, and John Dewey, and I am indebted to that periodical for the privilege of book publication.

EDWIN E. SLOSSON.

NEW YORK,
March 1, 1914.

CONTENTS

[xi]

LIST OF PORTRAITS

[xiii]

MAJOR PROPHETS OF TO-DAY

CHAPTER I

MAURICE MAETERLINCK

Let us not forget that we live in pregnant and decisive times. It is probable that our descendants will envy us the dawn through which, without knowing it, we are passing, just as we envy those who took part in the age of Pericles, in the most glorious days of Roman greatness and in certain hours of the Italian Renascence. The splendid dust that clouds the great movements of men shines brightly in the memory, but blinds those who raise it and breathe it, hiding from them the direction of their road and, above all, the thought, the necessity or the instinct that leads them. — "The Double Garden."

It was half past seven in the morning of my last possible day in Paris, when the maid brought on the tray with my chocolate, a blue envelope addressed in the business-like writing of Maeterlinck; the long expected and at last despaired of note confirming the invitation received in America to visit him at the Abbey of St. Wandrille, and setting five P.M. as the time. No chocolate for me that morning. The con-

[1]

cierge and I put our heads together over a French railway guide, more baffling than Bullinger's, and we made up our minds that a train started in that direction at nine, although where and when it made connections we neither of us could make out. From Rouen on, I would have to trust to luck, or to the Government railway service — much the same thing.

The Gare St. Lazare is a long way from the Latin Quarter when one has got to make a train, but the cabman said he would make it, and he did. At Rouen, I discovered that in the course of the day one could get to Barentin, and from Barentin, a deliberate and occasional train went to St. Wandrille. But when I got to Barentin I found that the train was not going till the following day. It was getting near tea time and Maeterlinck seventeen miles away! Barentin would, under other circumstances, have interested me on account of the incompatibility of temper between the town and its environment, a cotton-spinning, socialistic population in the midst of an ultra-Catholic agricultural community. But as I strolled about, I took no interest in anything until I came to a little automobile repair shop. Here I found a young man who knew where he could find a machine and promised to get me to St. Wandrille in time for tea, or burst a tire.

[2]

MAURICE MAETERLINCK

It was a joy ride certainly, in one sense of the word, and, I suspect, in two. The road, such a road as we rarely see in this country, wound around the hills overlooking the valley through which the Seine twisted its way to the sea. The banks were flooded with the July rains, and the poplars were up to their knees in water. We gradually left behind us the smart brick houses of the new cotton aristocracy, and came into the older stone age. Along the railroad, as I was sorry to see, the meadows were beginning to grow the most noxious of American weeds, big advertising signs, but we soon escaped them, and saw around us only the grass and fields through the double row of trees that lined the road.

As we got away from town, my extemporized chauffeur made better time, and under the stimulus of the acceleration, I recited passages of Maeterlinck's dithyramb to "Speed", for he was the first to perceive poetry in the automobile :

The pace grows faster and faster, the delirious wheels cry aloud in their gladness. And at first the road comes moving toward me, like a bride waving palms, rhythmically keeping time to some joyous melody. But soon it grows frantic, springs forward and throws itself madly upon me, rushing under the car like a furious torrent whose foam lashes my face. . . . Now the road drops sheer into the abyss, and the magical carriage rushes ahead of it. The

[3]

trees, that for so many slow-moving years have serenely dwelt on its borders, shrink back in dread of disaster. They seem to be hastening one to the other, to approach their green heads, and in startled groups to debate how to bar the way of the strange apparition. But as this rushes onward they take panic, and scatter and fly, each one quickly seeking its own habitual place; and as I pass they bend tumultuously forward, and their myriad leaves, quick to the mad joy of the force that is chanting its hymn, murmur in my ears the voluble psalm of space, acclaiming and greeting the enemy that hitherto has always been conquered but now at last triumphs: Speed.

Afterward, when I recalled this essay to Maeterlinck, he laughed heartily and said he had written it when he had only a three-horse power automobile, one of the first kind made and altogether unreliable. Now he has a big one; also a motor cycle with which he makes fifty miles an hour, but I do not know that he is writing prose poems on the motor cycle yet. He is likely to be the first to do it, though, unless Rostand or Kipling get ahead of him, as they have in literary aviation: Rostand with a sonnet on the biplane and Kipling with his "Night Mail", wherein he invents and teaches a new technical vocabulary without slackening speed. No wonder Kipling got the Nobel prize for idealistic literature. Maeterlinck, who received the same prize in 1911, deserved it on the same ground, for he, too, is entitled to write after his name the degree of M. M., Master of Machinery.

With the help of the machine, I got to the little village of St. Wandrille even before the appointed hour, so I had time to drop into the queer old church. This is a favorite resort of pilgrims from all over Normandy and not undeserving of its repute, if one may judge from the crutches, canes, and votive tablets left behind by those who have been cured or blessed. Ever since 684 A.D., when Wandregisilus left the French court and founded this retreat in the forest by the Seine, it has been noted for its relics. The ossuary department indeed makes a fine display; skulls, thigh bones, vertebræ, and phalanges, all laid out under glass and labeled neatly, as in a museum. Thirty saints I counted, some familiar like St. Thomas Aquinas, St. Clotilde, St. Genevieve, and St. Wulfranc. But most of those represented by relics or wooden statues were quite outside the range of my hagiography — St. Firmin, St. Mien, St. Vilmir, St. Wilgeforte, St. Pantoleon, and St. Herbland.

The village church is too modern to interest any one but an American. The old abbey, dating in part from the twelfth century, and belonging now

[5]

to Maeterlinck, is across the road. Ringing at the little arched portal in the wall, I was shown into the cloister; very familiar it seemed to me, for I had a photograph of it in my room at home, a photograph showing three witches over a caldron, since it was taken when Maeterlinck's version of "Macbeth" was played here. "The cloister of St. Wandrille is without doubt one of the most magnificent monuments of the kind that has escaped the vandalism of recent times", says Langlois in the large volume he devoted to its architecture.[1] Until recently the monastery was in the hands of the Benedictines, but they were dispossessed by the French Government on the separation of Church and State in 1907, and the property offered for sale. It was about to be sold to a chemical syndicate for a factory, when Maeterlinck intervened and purchased it, possibly more to please his wife than himself, for he is indifferent to surroundings, while she takes a keen delight in an artistic stage setting, not merely for the plays she enacts, but for daily life. For thus saving the abbey from commercial desecration, Maeterlinck received a parchment blessing from the Pope, but his later use of it as a theater was quite as offensive to Catholic sentiment.

---

[1] "L'Abbaye de Fontenelle ou de Saint-Wandrille." Paris. 1827.

MAURICE MAETERLINCK

Certainly no author has been housed more satisfactorily to his admirers than Maeterlinck. He had, in fact, pictured it in his youthful plays. It is a verification of his faith that a man creates his own environment. The surrounding forest, the old house with its long corridors, the garden where the broken pillars and arches of the buried temple appear here and there among the vines and flowers, are the familiar scenes of all his dramas. All that is lacking is the sea, which is so often in his thoughts, and some dank, dark caves and dungeons underneath. But Maeterlinck does not need nowadays such subterranean accessories, for he has passed through his Reign of Terror, and come up into the sunshine.

It is curious that a man who is so modernistic in mind and who has shown so unique a power to idealize the prosaic details of the life of to-day, should place all his dramas in the historical or legendary past. But he always views the past as a poet, not as an archæologist, giving merely some beautiful names and a suggestion as to scene setting, and leaving it to the imagination of the reader to do the stage carpentering. Determinist though he is, no one, not even James or Bergson, has been more bold in repudiating the right of the past to control our actions :

In reality, if we think of it, the past belongs to us quite as much as the present, and is far more malleable than the future. Like the present, and to a much greater extent than the future, its existence is all in our thoughts, and our hand controls it; nor is this true only of our material past, wherein there are ruins that we perhaps can restore, but also of those regions that are closed to our tardy desire for atonement, and, above all, of our moral past, and of what we consider to be most irreparable there.

"The past is past", we say, and it is not true; the past is always present. "We have to bear the burden of our past", we sigh; and it is not true; the past bears our burden. "Nothing can wipe out the past", and it is not true; the least effort of will sends present and future traveling over the past, to efface whatever we bid them efface. "The indestructible, irreparable, immutable past!" And that is no truer than the rest. In those who speak thus it is the present that is immutable and knows not how to repair. "My past is wicked, it is sorrowful, empty", we say again, "as I look back I can see no moment of beauty, or happiness or love; I see nothing but wretched ruins. . . ." And that is not true, for you behold precisely what you yourself place there at the moment your eyes rest upon it.[1]

While I was wandering in the cloister, puzzling over battered saints and mossy gargoyles, any disposition I may have felt toward monastic meditation was dissipated by the appearance of a woman, not merely a woman, but a modern woman, one who has

[1] From "The Past", by Maurice Maeterlinck. *The Independent,* March 6, 1902.

gained vitality and initiative without losing the feminine graces, "the virile friend and equal comrade", as Maeterlinck calls her. Her costume was not inharmonious with the surroundings, for it was vaguely medieval in appearance — a hooded robe of some heavy blue stuff, falling in long straight folds to her feet.

It is not necessary to describe Madame Georgette Leblanc Maeterlinck, for Maeterlinck himself has done that, sketching equally her virtues and failings with a loving hand.[1] Her powerful influence over his thought he gratefully acknowledges in the prefaces to his essays, and shows it by the frequent references in them to her opinions and personality. Monna Vanna, Joyzelle, and Mary Magdalene are rôles written for her. We can tell when she came into Maeterlinck's life by the appearance of "the new woman" in his dramas; Aglavaine, who involuntarily overshadows and displaces the frail and timid Sélysette, Ariane, the last wife of Blue Beard, who releases his other wives from the secret chamber where they were confined, not killed as earlier rumor had it. The imprisoned sisterhood, who are, by the way, the anæmic heroines of Maeterlinck's earlier period, Sélysette, Mélisande, Ygraine, Bellangère,

---

[1] "The Portrait of a Lady", in "The Double Garden."

and Alladine, refuse to follow Ariane to freedom; they prefer to stay with Blue Beard, so she goes out alone. But she does not slam the door like Nora in "The Doll's House." It is not necessary nowadays to slam the door.

Madame Maeterlinck shows me the places she picked out for the scenes of "Pelléas and Mélisande", for she is the inventor of a new form of dramatic art based on the discovery that audiences are easier moved about than castles, trees, and hills. Only the weather she cannot control, and the pathetic drama was played appropriately though inconveniently in a rainstorm.[1] The ancient refectory which she used as the banquet hall in "Macbeth" was large enough to seat four hundred Benedictine monks at table. It is roofed and paneled with carved wood and lighted by a row of large pointed windows set with bits of very old stained glass.

Here we are soon joined by M. Maeterlinck, a sturdy figure in Norfolk jacket and knickerbockers, for he is just in from a tramp in the woods with his dog. No, the dog was not his friend, Pelléas. Pelléas, as you should have remembered, died years ago, very young.

[1] See her account of the performance in *Century Magazine*, January, 1911.

MAURICE MAETERLINCK

Some say that Maeterlinck has a Flemish peasant face. Some say a Flemish bourgeois face. Not being familiar with the physiognomy of either the peasantry or the bourgeoisie of Flanders, I cannot decide this delicate question. All I can say is that it is a face one could trust, the face of a man one would like to have for a friend. The eyes, wide open and wide apart, are clear and steady. His hair is getting gray, and he has in recent years shaved off his mustache, showing his straight, firm-set mouth and pleasant smile. His photographs do not do him justice, for none of them show him smiling — neither do his books. Early to bed and early to rise and much time spent in the open air have given him an erect carriage and a vigorous step. He is fond of boxing and has written an essay in praise of this sport.

From the window of his study upstairs he points out to me his woodland stretching far up the hill, and he takes from his pocket the book that has occupied his afternoon, a book of trout flies. But I am more interested in other things, in the big work-table that occupies the center of the study, littered with papers, a typewriter on the corner of it. The wall opposite the window is lined with books, and as I glance over them I see his own plays and essays translated into half a dozen languages, Carlyle's works, Vaughan's "English Mystics", and many volumes of natural science, poetry, and philosophy. M. Maeterlinck divines what I want most to see and takes down his Emerson, an old one-volume edition, in excruciatingly fine print, but manifestly well read, with numerous underlinings and as much annotation as the narrow margins would permit. It is curious that Emerson should have strongly influenced two such unlike men as Nietzsche and Maeterlinck.[1] But only the latter acquired his finest attribute, serenity of spirit. Maeterlinck also resembles Thoreau in his love for nature, though he makes no affectation of asceticism or hermitage.

He spends his summers only at the Abbaye de St. Wandrille. In the winter he goes to the Riviera, to live with the bees and the flowers whose language he speaks. His winter residence is at Les Quatre Chemins, near Grasse, in the southeastern corner of the country. Here he is even more secluded than at St. Wandrille. He prefers the country to the city, not because he has any aversion to people in mass or to the mechanism of modern life, but because he dislikes lionization and publicity of all

[1] For Maeterlinck on Emerson, see *Poet Lore*, Vol. 10, p. 76, January, 1898, and *Arena*, Vol. 16, p. 563, March, 1896.

sorts. He would stifle in the atmosphere of a Parisian salon. He belongs to none of the literary coteries combined for mutual admiration and the reciprocal promotion of individual interests. He has never been what Verlaine used to call a "Cymbalist."

As a mystic philosopher Maeterlinck finds a flower in a crannied wall sufficient to give him a clew to the secrets of the universe. Modern science, instead of killing mysticism, as was foreboded by despairing poets of the last century, has brought about a revival of it. This is quite natural, for mysticism is the verification of religion by the experimental method, as ecclesiasticism is the verification of religion by the historical method. The doctrine of evolution has given an intellectual basis and a richer content to the sense of the unity of nature, which is the force of mysticism. A weak poet, distrustful of his vision or of his own powers, fears science and flees from it. A great and courageous poet seizes science and turns it to his own uses. Tennyson and Sully-Prudhomme were among the first to perceive and to demonstrate the possibility of this. Maeterlinck, being of the generation born since the dawn of the scientific era, entered upon the inheritance of its wealth without having to pass through any storm and stress period to acquire it.

No traces of the fretful antagonisms of the nineteenth century disturb the equanimity of his essays. He sees no conflict between the scientific and poetic views of the world. He looks upon it with both eyes open and the two visions fuse into one solid reality.

Maeterlinck has been a leader in that characteristic movement of the twentieth century which might be called the reanimation of the universe. Time was, and was not so long ago but that most of us can remember it, when, terrified by the advance of science, man did not dare to call his soul his own. Naturally he denied a soul to the rest of the world. Animals were automatons; plants, of course, unconscious; and planets and machines out of the question. Nature was subjected to a process succinctly to be described as deanthropomorphization. To naturalists of the inanimate school an insect was not worth studying until it had a pin through it. Animals were only interesting when stuffed.

Nowadays naturalists are going back to nature. They are leaving the laboratory for the woods. They have come to realize that studying zoölogy in a museum is like studying sociology in a cemetery. They have discovered that animals and plants possess not merely vitality, but individuality, and since man's real interest in the world he looks down upon has always been, though he has often denied it, because he hoped to see himself there, a new school of fabulists has appeared who hold the mirror of nature up to us as Esop and Pilpay did of old.

Among them there is no one, unless it be Kipling, who is the equal of Maeterlinck. Like Tyltyl, he wears the fairy button on his cap which, when touched, brings out the souls of things. And, as in "The Blue Bird", the souls he has once released by the magic of his phrases from their material prisons do not get back again. They remain visible to us ever after; not merely the souls of the dog and the cat, but of the bee, the oak, the bread, and the automobile. He shows us the cat as a diminutive but undomesticated tiger to whom we are nothing more than an overgrown and uneatable prey. We see through his eyes the cultivated plants as our dumb slaves, for "the rose and the corn, had they wings, would fly at our approach like the birds."

Maeterlinck has recently been testing the thinking horses of Eberfeld, the successors of Kluge Hans, and convinced himself of their ability to spell and cipher, even to extract the square root of big numbers, a feat which Maeterlinck says he himself could never learn at school. He does, however, draw the line at crediting the horses with telepathic powers.[1]

"The Blue Bird" cannot escape comparison with its contemporary rival on the stage, "Chantecler", but the similarity is superficial. They are as unlike in their philosophy as in their style. Maeterlinck has written a fairy story for children; Rostand a satire for grown people. Maeterlinck conceals his depth of thought under a dialogue of simple and artless prose. Rostand disguises his trivialities in elaborate and artificial versification. "The Blue Bird" is really the offspring of "The Little White Bird", Mendel to the contrary notwithstanding. But Maeterlinck lacks the delicious humor with which Barrie had depicted his Peter Pan.

Whether one who has read "The Blue Bird" will be disappointed when he sees it depends upon the vividness of his imagination. He will probably find that he has in reading it failed to appreciate the humor of the grotesque characterization of the minor characters, such as the Bread, Dog, Cat, and Sugar, but on the other hand he will find that he has pictured to himself such scenes as the Palace of Night and the Kingdom of the Future much more splendid and impressive than they appear on the

[1] *Metropolitan Magazine*, May, 1914.

stage. The play as performed at the New Theater in New York was not nearly so effective as at the Haymarket in London.

"The Blue Bird" would go best as an opera. I wish somebody would set it to music. The very impressive song of the mothers welcoming their children shows how much music might add to it. Débussy's dreamy and formless harmonies suited "Pelléas and Mélisande", but the author of the "Domestic Symphony" alone could do justice to this kitchen drama. Only Strauss could fit Sugar and Milk with suitable motives, and give the proper orchestration to the quarrels of Cat and Dog, and Fire and Water.

With Maeterlinck, personification is not accomplished through falsification. His "Life of the Bee" is based on his own observation and wide reading, and is freer from error than many of the purely scientific books written on the subject. Such mistakes in fact, as he makes, are accidental and never due to distortion or invention for the purpose of working in a poetic fancy or of pointing a moral. In fact, he does not point a moral. His nature studies teach no lesson unless it is the great lesson of kinship with nature. He does not, like Kipling, write an animal story with the aim of amending the

[17]

budget bill or changing diplomatic relations. "The Life of the Bee" may be used as a socialistic tract. It may also be used as an anti-socialistic tract. "The spirit of the hive", as he interprets it, attracts some people and repels others. Lord Avebury, who is the leading English authority on ants and bees, is the head of the society for opposing socialism.

Maeterlinck is not one of those who set up animals on their hind legs to act as schoolmasters to men. He finds nowhere outside of ourselves, neither in the heavens above nor in the earth beneath, that justice in which mankind instinctively and inevitably believes. He is as largely pragmatic as Sumner in his derivation of morality :

Between the external world and our actions there exists only the simple and essentially non-moral relations of cause and effect.

In the course of adapting ourselves to the laws of life we have naturally been led to credit with our moral ideas those principles of causality that we encounter most frequently. And we have in this fashion created a very plausible semblance of effective justice, which rewards or punishes most of our actions in the degree that they approach, or deviate from, certain laws that are essential for the preservation of the race.

Within us there is a spirit that weighs only intentions; without us a power that only balances deeds.[1]

[1] "The Mystery of Justice", in "The Double Garden."

MAURICE MAETERLINCK

This reads like a twentieth century supplement to Huxley's Romanes address.

Maeterlinck's sense of justice is more outraged by the calamities that result from the carelessness and malevolence of man than the disasters of earthquake and tempest. We are strange lovers of an ideal justice, he says; we who condemn three fourths of mankind to the misery of poverty and disease, and then complain of the injustice of impersonal nature. And in reading a story of the "Arabian Nights", he is struck by the fact that the women of the harem, creatures trained to vice and condemned to slavery, give utterance to the highest moral precepts:

These women, who forever are pondering the loftiest, grandest problems of justice, of the morality of men and of nations, never throw one questioning glance on their own fate, or for one instant suspect the abominable injustice whereof they are victims. Nor do those suspect it either who listen to them, and love and admire and understand them. And we who marvel at this — we who also reflect on justice and virtue, on pity and love — are we so sure that they who come after us shall not some day find in our present social condition a spectacle equally disconcerting and amazing.[1]

Maeterlinck stands quite aloof from politics, but not because he is out of sympathy with the tendency

[1] *The Independent*, January 3, 1901.

of the times. He has faith in democracy in spite of his clear perception of its faults and dangers:

In those problems in which all life's enigmas converge, the crowd which is wrong is almost always justified as against the wise man who is right. It refuses to believe him on his word. It feels dimly that behind the most evident abstract truths there are numberless living truths which no brain can foresee, for they need time, reality and men's passions to develop their work. That is why, whatever warning we may give it, whatever prediction we may make to it, the crowd insists before all that the experiment shall be tried. Can we say that, in cases where the crowd has obtained the experiment, it was wrong to insist upon it? [1]

It would surely have been highly dangerous to confide the destinies of the species to Plato or Aristotle, Marcus Aurelius, Shakespeare or Montesquieu. At the very worst moments of the French Revolution the fate of the people was in the hands of philosophers of no mean order. [2]

The thoroughgoing character of his democracy is emphasized by Professor Dewey in his lecture on "Maeterlinck's Philosophy of Life" delivered at Columbia University:

"Emerson, Walt Whitman, and Maeterlinck are thus far, perhaps, the only men who have been habitually, and, as it were, instinctively, aware that democracy is neither a form of government nor a

[1] "The Double Garden."   [2] "The Mystery of Justice."

social expediency, but a metaphysic of the relation
of man and his experience to nature; among these
Maeterlinck has at least the advantage of greater
illumination by the progress of natural science."

This democratic feeling seems to me to arise more
from his mystical sense of the continuity of life
than from personal disposition or political theory.
In his earlier and more characteristic dramas, the
persons are hardly more than talking symbols.
Their looks and costumes are not described, either
in the stage directions or in the dialogue. Their
names — if he takes the trouble to give them names
— are scarcely sufficient in some cases to indicate
the sex. Their speech is language reduced to its
lowest elements, excessively simplified, in fact,
and full of the repetitions and incoherencies common to stupid and uneducated people the world
over. Maeterlinck himself calls them "marion-
nettes", and says that they have the appearance of
half deaf somnambulists just awakening from a
painful dream.

But these puppet people are divested of individuality for the purpose of reducing them to the common
denominator of humanity. They are devoided of
personal interest in order to prevent the attention
of the spectator from being fixed upon them. They

are made transparent so that we may look through them and perceive the external forces which control them. The dramatic poet, he says in the preface to his early dramas, "must show us in what way, in what form, in what conditions, according to what laws, and to what end our destinies are controlled by the superior powers, the unintelligible influences, the infinite principles of which, in so far as he is a poet, he is persuaded that the universe is full."

Great poetry he regards as composed of three principal elements:

First, verbal beauty, then the contemplation and passionate depiction of what really exists around us and in ourselves, that is to say, nature and feeling, and, finally, enveloping the entire work and creating its own atmosphere, the idea which the poet has of the unknown in which float the beings and things he evokes, of the mystery which dominates them and judges them and presides over their destinies.

The critics were not altogether wrong when they called the characters of his earlier plays "mere shadows." But a shadow exists only when a bright light is cast on a real object. Maeterlinck's purpose is to make Plato's cave men aware of the drama that is being enacted behind their backs. The real action of these plays is not that seen on the stage. His dramas contain their message written in secret ink between the lines, and it becomes visible only when warmed by the sympathy of the reader.

The performance of "Macbeth" at Saint-Wandrille had a double interest. It introduced a novel form of the drama, and it added another to the many attempts to put Shakespeare into French. This select and household entertainment might be called "chamber pageantry", because it bears somewhat the same relation to the outdoor processionings now so popular as chamber music does to orchestral. Most of the incongruities which the critics pointed out [1] are not inherent in the plan, but due to the fact that "Macbeth" is not adapted to such a setting any more than it is to the modern theater. Conceivably something more effective could be done in this line if a new play were written to fit the place and the conditions of enactment, requirements certainly not more exigeant than those of the Elizabethan stage. In this it would even be possible to keep strictly to the three unities, and play the scenes appropriately indoors and out, in daylight and dark.

Madame Georgette Leblanc-Maeterlinck has been, as wives are apt to be, both a help and a hindrance to her husband. She has inspired some of his best

---

[1] For a description of the performance see "A Realization of Macbeth" by Alvan G. Sanborn in *The Independent*, September 15, 1909.

work and also embroiled him in interminable controversies with theatrical managers. "Monna Vanna" was written for her, so, very naturally, she wanted a monopoly of the title rôle, and when Débussy set "Pelléas et Mélisande" to music as unearthly as the play, she insisted upon singing Mélisande. But the Parisian managers, either because they had *protégées* of their own or because they did not have a sufficiently high opinion of Madame Leblanc's capabilities as an actress and a prima donna, declined to take her, and M. Maeterlinck was not able to compel them to, or to prevent the production of the play and opera with other leading ladies. She did, however, finally sing the part both at home and in America, though she lost the distinction of creating it.

But, at any rate, we owe to her assiduity a new translation of "Macbeth", which the London *Times* says "is the most conscientious effort to preserve the atmosphere of a Shakespearean play which has been attempted in French since M. Marcel Schwab's remarkable rendering of 'Hamlet.'" The difficulty of translating poetical language, wherein the sound and connotation of the words are as essential as their literal meaning, is admirably stated by M. Maeterlinck:

MAURICE MAETERLINCK

The humble translators face to face with Shakespeare are like painters seated in front of the same forest, the same seas, on the same mountain. Each of them will make a different picture. And a translation is almost as much an *état d'âme* as is a landscape. Above, below, and all round the literal and literary sense of the primitive phrase floats a secret life which is all but impossible to catch, and which is, nevertheless, more important than the external life of the words and of the images. It is that secret life which it is important to understand and to reproduce as well one can. Extreme prudence is required, since the slightest false note, the smallest error, may destroy the illusion and destroy the beauty of the finest page. Such is the ideal of the conscientious translator. It excuses in advance every effort of the kind, even this one, which comes after so many others, and contributes to the common work merely the very modest aid of a few phrases which chance may now and then have favored.

He illustrates these variant views of the same landscape by bringing together all the different versions of a couplet, from Letourneur of the eighteenth century to Duval, the latest translator of Shakespeare :

"Strange things I have in head that will to hand
Which must be acted ere they may be scann'd."

"J'ai dans la tête d'étranges choses qui aboutiront à ma main ; et qu'il faut accomplir avant qu'on les médite." — (Maeterlinck.)
"J'ai dans la tête d'étranges choses qui réclament

ma main et veulent être exécutées avant d'être méditées." — (François-Victor Hugo.)

"Ma tête a des projets étranges qui réclament ma main; achevons l'acte avant d'y réfléchir." — (Maurice Pottecher.)

"J'ai dans la tête d'étranges choses qui passeront dans mes mains, des choses qu'il faut exécuter avant d'avoir le temps de les examiner." — (Guizot.)

"J'ai dans ma tête d'étranges choses que ma main executera, et qui veulent être accomplies sans me laisser le temps de les peser." — (Montégut.)

"Ma tête a des projets qu'exécutera ma main; je veux les accomplir de suite, sans me donner le temps de les examiner de trop près." — (Benjamin Laroche.)

"J'ai d'étranges projets en tête qui veulent être exécutés avant d'y réfléchir." — (Georges Duval.)

"J'ai dans la tête d'étranges projets, qui, de là, passeront dans mes mains; et il faut les exécuter avant qu'on puisse les pénétrer." — (Pierre Letourneur.)

This couplet is in itself an argument for more freedom of translation than is customarily allowed. The choice of "scann'd" from among other words that would have expressed the idea as well or better was obviously dictated by the necessity of rhyming with "hand", and this in turn was due to the desire to alliterate with "head." A translator, if he is to make as good poetry as the original author, must have an equal license. It is therefore not surprising to see that M. Maeterlinck

has been most successful in preserving the spirit
of the original where he has translated into rhyme
instead of prose, for here the exactions of the French
verse have forced him to a greater freedom. Here
are fragments of the witches' songs :

Paddock crie, "Allez, allez."
Le laid est beau et le beau laid
Allons flotter dans la brume,
Allons faire le tour du monde,
Dans la brume et l'air immonde.

Trois fois le chat miaula
Le hérisson piaula.
Harpier crie, "Voilà ! voilà !"

Double, double, puis redouble,
Le feu chante au chaudron trouble.

In order that the reader may judge for himself
whether the Belgian poet has succeeded in this
effort to put Shakespeare into French, we quote a
few passages of especial difficulty. The complete
text is published in *Illustration* of August 28, 1909.

Et, enfin, ce Duncan fut si doux sur son trône,
si pur dans sa puissance que ses vertues parleront
comme d'angéliques trompettes contre le crime
damné de son assassinat. Et la pitié, pareille à un
nouveau-né chevauchant la tempête, ou à un cheru-
bin céleste qui monte les coursiers invisibles de l'air,
soufflerait l'acte horrible ·dans les yeux de tout
homme jusqu' à noyer le vent parmi les larmes.

[27]

"Tu ne dormiras ! Macbeth a tué le sommeil !"
L'innocent sommeil, le sommeil qui dévide l'écheveau
embrouillé des soucis.

Tout l'océan du grand Neptune pourrait-il
laver ce sang de ma main ? Non, c'est plutôt
cette main qui empourprera les vagues innombrables,
faisant de la mer verte un océan rouge.

Maeterlinck has himself suffered many things
of many translators. Alfred Sutro has given us
admirable versions of his philosophical works, "Wisdom and Destiny", "The Treasure of the Humble",
and "The Life of the Bee", but his plays have not
been so fortunate, for their emotional effect is dependent upon the maintenance of a peculiar atmosphere, so sensitive that a harsh breath will destroy
it, leaving ridiculous wooden puppets where the
moment before we thought we glimpsed beings of
supernatural beauty. So even a reader whose
French is feeble will prefer the plays in the original,
for their language is of extreme simplicity and the
effect may be even enhanced by the additional veil
that his partial incomprehension draws across the
stage picture. Then, too, Maeterlinck's trick of
triple repetition which offends our Anglo-Saxon
ears ceases to annoy us in French, for in that language
even identical rhymes are permissible.

As an example of how a prosaic literalism may

spoil the illusion, let us take that exquisite passage which closes "Pelléas et Mélisande":

C'était un petit être si tranquille, si timide et si silencìeux. C'était un pauvre petit être mysterìeux, comme tout le monde. Elle est là, comme si elle était la grande sœur de son enfant.

This is the way it is rendered by Laurence Alma Tadema, and the libretto of the opera is still worse:

" It was a little gentle being, so quiet, so timid and so silent. It was a poor little mysterious being, like all the world. She lies there as if she were her own child's big sister."

The wise old man, who at Mélisande's death bed sums up her character in the words, *"C'était un pauvre petit être mysterieux, comme tout le monde"*, gives at the same time the key to the philosophy of the play. — "She was a poor little mysterious being like every one." "Like every one"! The phrase throws back a level ray of light, as though it were a setting sun, and illuminates the dark road we have traversed. "Like every one", and all this while we had been thinking what an unnatural and absurd creature this Mélisande was, this princess who did not know where she came from or where she was going to, who was always weeping without reason, who played so carelessly with her wedding ring over the well's mouth, and whose words could never express what she felt. "Like every one"? perhaps . . . at any rate to be thought on, once it has been suggested to us. And in this connection we may consider a sentence in "Wisdom and Destiny":

Genius only throws into bolder relief all that can and actually does take place in the lives of all men; otherwise were it genius no longer but incoherence or madness.

What fun Francisque Sarcey did make of "Pelléas and Mélisande" and of its admirers at its first representation in Paris in 1893. According to the veteran critic of *Le Temps*,[1] the play contained a triple symbolism; one part not understood by the profane, one part not understood by the initiates, and one part not understood by the author. Maeterlinck was only a passing craze, he thought, due to the reprehensible fondness of the Parisians for anything foreign. Yet some fifteen years after that he might have seen in New York blocks of people standing for hours in the snow around the Manhattan Opera House to get a chance to see, with the added charm of Débussy's music, this same play that the critics called "Maeterlinck's Sedan."

Even Richard Hovey, who first introduced Maeter-

[1] See his "Quarante Ans de Théâtre."

linck's plays to America in the days when the "Green Tree Library" flourished and bore its strange fruit, feared that "his devotion to the wormy side of things may prevent him from ever becoming popular." But he got over his devotion to the wormy side of things and has grown into a more wholesome philosophy and so into a greater popularity. The transition point in his style and thought is marked by the preface to his dramas, 1901. He neither recants nor apologizes for his earlier work, still less does he ridicule it, as Ruskin did his first writing, but he frankly and gracefully indicates the changed attitude toward life which shows itself in his later essays.

He ceases to use the word "destiny" exclusively in its evil sense, and to represent it as a power inimical to man, watching in the shadow to pounce upon us whenever we manifest a little joy. Fate in his later work does not always mean fatality, and events are controlled by character more than by external forces. Man by wisdom can overcome destiny. But Maeterlinck would have us take care to keep a sane balance of altruism and egoism:

You are told you should love your neighbor as yourself; but if you love yourself meanly, childishly, timidly, even so shall you love your neighbor. Learn, therefore, to love yourself with a love that is wise and healthy, that is large and complete.

It is a curious transformation by which this Belgian lawyer and esoteric poet has become one of the widest known of French playwrights and moralists. He was born in Ghent, August 29, 1862, of an old Flemish family. The name, "measurer of grain", is derived from an ancestor who was generous in a time of famine.

He was educated at the University of Ghent for law, in accordance with the wishes of his family, though he would have preferred medicine. But his dominant interest was always literature.

His experience at the bar was brief, a couple of criminal cases, and then he deserted the law and went to Paris for a year, where he was chiefly under the influence of the French symbolist, Villiers de l'Isle-Adam. Then he returned home to devote himself in quiet to the cultivation of his double garden of literature and science. He was especially attracted by the freshness and richness of Shakespeare and his contemporaries, and, as he says, drank long and thirstily from the Elizabethan springs. In Shelley and Browning he was also deeply interested.[1]

[1] His admiration for Browning appears in his reply to Professor William Lyon Phelps, of Yale, who had called attention to the close similarity between an incident in Browning's "Luria" and Maeterlinck's "Monna Vanna." Maeterlinck very frankly and courteously acknowledged his indebtedness to Browning, whom, he said, he regarded, like Eschylus,

MAURICE MAETERLINCK

At the age of twenty-four he began to contribute to *La Pléiade*, the organ of the "Young Belgians", a group of ambitious young writers, impressionists, seekers after novel effects of style, chiefly attained by means of transferring descriptive adjectives from one of the five senses to the other four. In the third number of this short-lived periodical was published Maeterlinck's first and apparently his last story, "The Massacre of the Innocents", a biblical incident reset in the times of the Spanish wars.[1] Here appeared some of the poems republished in 1889 in the little volume entitled "Serres Chaudes" ("Hot-house Blooms").

The cross-fertilization of Elizabethan drama with French symbolism gave rise to the "Princess Maleine", a new species if there ever was one, Shakespearean in form and incident, most un-Shakespearean in everything else. The first edition of this drama was an extremely limited one, twenty copies, printed on a hand press with Maeterlinck turning the crank.

Sophocles, and Shakespeare, as common sources of literary inspiration. *The Independent*, March 5 and June 11, 1903.

[1] This is signed by his name in its original form, Mooris Mäterlinck. A translation of this and other tales by Belgian writers by Edith Wingate Rinder was published in 1897 in the "Green Tree Library" of Stone & Kimball (now Duffield & Co.).

It was the "Princess Maleine" which led to his "discovery" by Octave Mirbeau, who proclaimed it "the greatest work of genius of the times", and "superior in beauty to what is most beautiful in Shakespeare." [1] This newspaper praise made Maeterlinck instantly famous everywhere save in his own country. His neighbors in Ghent refused to take it seriously, and thought it a pity that his family should encourage the young man in his mania by paying for puffs like that.

To trace Maeterlinck's dramatic development is like watching a materialization at a séance. His characters have become increasingly solid and life-like, but they have lost the illusiveness and allusiveness that made their charm in his earlier plays. Maeterlinck has never been able to equal Ibsen —— nor has any one else — in the art of making a perfectly individualized and natural character serve also as a type or symbol, thus doubling our interest by combining the specific and the general.

Maeterlinck's genius shows best in his own peculiar field of symbolism and suggestion, that of his early dramas and of "The Blue Bird." His plays of a

<hr>

[1] *Figaro*, August 24, 1890. Octave Mirbeau later busied himself in booming Marguerite Audoux, the Paris sempstress, who wrote "Marie-Claire."

more conventional type, "Monna Vanna" and "Mary Magdalene", betray his deficiencies as a dramatic writer, his lack of the power of plot construction and a sense of humor. "Mary Magdalene" is really as much a one-act play as "The Interior", for the last act is the only one that counts. Here the crowd has the star part, the crowd of the lame, the halt and the blind, the sinners and the diseased, whom Jesus has cured and who now desert him; and the real drama is enacted, not in the upper chamber of the house of Joseph of Arimathea, but in the street outside, leading to the Place of the Skull. The scene of the woman taken in adultery is far less dramatic than in its biblical form, because in the play she is really protected by Roman swords, not by the awakened consciences of the mob.

The continuous development of Maeterlinck's philosophy of life is shown as well in his plays as in his essays. Mary Magdalene, who would not save her Savior by the sacrifice of her virtue, represents a higher ethical ideal than Monna Vanna, who gives herself for the city. In his earlier plays Maeterlinck tries to frighten us with the traditional Terrors which in "The Blue Bird" are shown to be imprisoned and harmless in the Palace of Night. Old Time with his scythe, who as "The Intruder" of twenty years ago brought death into the household, appears now in "The Blue Bird" under a kinder aspect, calling the Children of the Future into life. In fact, "The Blue Bird" represents the highest point of the philosophy of optimism, for it is based upon the most daring of all the assumptions of science — that the secret of existence is also the secret of happiness. "To be wise is above all to be happy", says Maeterlinck. Truly, he has got a long way from Schopenhauer, the object of his boyish admiration.

Maeterlinck has, in short, acquired a faith. I do not see exactly whom or what he has faith in, but he has faith, and that, after all, seems to be the main thing. The development of his thought has an especial interest in that it shows how a spiritual interpretation of the universe and a moral support can be built up on pure agnosticism. From Christianity he has derived little except a vague symbolism and certain ethical ideals. He looks back with bitterness upon his school days in the Jesuit college at Ghent, but his writings show no trace of the anticlerical animosity which is so conspicuous in Haeckel's. It was his latest book, "Death", the most religious of them all, breathing a spirit of unconquerable faith in immortality and future happiness, that brought down upon Maeterlinck the condemnation of Rome, and in 1914 all his books and plays were put upon the Index by the Sacred Congregation.

From the mystics he has derived much, especially from the German Novalis and the Flemish Ruysbroek, whose works he has translated into French. In his preface to the latter he says:

Mystical truths have this strange superiority over truths of the ordinary kind, that they know neither age nor death. . . . They possess the immunity of Swedenborg's angels, who progress continually toward the springtime of youth, so that the eldest angels always appear the youngest.

But he undoubtedly owes his ethical and philosophical growth most of all to the study of nature, not the vague contemplation of natural objects which in the early Victorian era was thought proper pabulum for poets, but the effort to understand nature through the use of modern scientific methods. We are reminded of Sir Thomas Browne, who says: "Those strange and mystical transmigrations that I have observed in silkworms turned my philosophy into divinity."

The reason why many poets and imaginative writers of high ability find themselves without influence in the modern world is, in my opinion, because they are ignorant of science or inimical to it.

They, therefore, write for antiquity, which does not buy books, or for posterity, which, it is safe to say, will never come back to the position they hold. The people do not enjoy science, but their manner of thought is molded by it, and they are unaffected or repelled by music out of tune with it.

Maeterlinck, while thoroughly appreciating science, does not exaggerate its power. He does not look to it for a complete explanation of the world.

Rarely does a mystery disappear; ordinarily it only changes its place. But it is often very important, very desirable, that it manage to change its place. From a certain point of view, all the progress of human thought reduces itself to two or three changes of this kind — to have dislodged two or three mysteries from the place where they did harm in order to transport them where they become harmless, where they can do good. Sometimes it is enough, without a mystery changing its place, if we can succeed in giving it another name. That which was called "the gods" is now called "life." And if life is just as inexplicable as the gods, we have at least gained this, that in the name of life no one has authority to speak nor right to do harm.

Maeterlinck does not seem to me so much an original thinker as an exquisitely sensitive personality who is able to catch the dominant note of the times in which he lives, and to give it artistic expression, as a musician upon a high tower might take as his

key the fundamental tone of the streets below, modu-
lating his music as the rhythm of the city changes,
not to obtain applause, but because his soul is in
sympathy with the life around him. In Maeterlinck's writings, various though they be in form
and topic, may be continuously traced the changing moods of the philosophy of the last twenty years,
for he has always retained his sincerity of thought
and courage of expression.

To look fearlessly upon life; to accept the laws
of nature, not with meek resignation, but as her sons,
who dare to search and question; to have peace
and confidence within our soul — these are the beliefs that make for happiness. But to believe is
not enough; all depends on how we believe. I may
believe that there is no God, that I am self-contained,
that my brief sojourn here serves no purpose; that
in the economy of this world without limit my existence counts for as little as the evanescent hue of a
flower — I may believe all this, in a deeply religious
spirit, with the infinite throbbing within me; you
may believe in one all-powerful God, who cherishes
and protects you, yet your belief may be mean, and
petty, and small. I shall be happier than you, and
calmer, if my doubt is greater, and nobler, and more
earnest than is your faith; if it has probed more
deeply into my soul, traversed wider horizons, if
there are more things it has loved. And if the
thoughts and feelings on which my doubt reposes
have become vaster and purer than those that support your faith, then shall the God of my disbelief

become mightier and of supremer comfort than the God to whom you cling. For, indeed, belief and unbelief are mere empty words; not so the loyalty, the greatness and profoundness of the reasons wherefore we believe or do not believe.[1]

HOW TO READ MAETERLINCK

To those familiar with Maeterlinck, the following, and perhaps also the foregoing, will be of no interest. But those who wish to make his closer acquaintance may find some suggestions not impertinent.

Maeterlinck's essays are published in English by Dodd, Mead and Company, in seven volumes: "The Treasure of the Humble"; "Wisdom and Destiny"; "The Buried Temple"; "The Measure of the Hours"; "The Double Garden"; "On Emerson and Other Essays" (Novalis and Ruysbroek); and "Our Eternity." The order given is that of their publication in French. Any one of them will give the reader an insight into the character of his thought; "Wisdom and Destiny" is the most consecutive. If one has time for but a single essay, he may read "The Leaf of Olive."

For his treatment of nature, see "The Life of the Bee" (Dodd, Mead and Company), essays in "The Double Garden" and in "The Measure of the Hours", and "The Insect's Homer" in *Forum*, September, 1910; also "News of Spring and Other Nature Studies", illustrated by E. J. Detmold (Dodd, Mead and Company).

[1] "Wisdom and Destiny," § 79.

MAURICE MAETERLINCK

Of his dramatic work the early mystical plays are most characteristic. The timid reader should avoid reading them alone after dark. Yet there is nothing supernatural in them — except the sense of the supernatural that permeates them. Nothing happens that cannot be given a rationalistic explanation — only the reader is not disposed at the time to accept such an explanation. Select your co-readers with care (all plays should, of course, be read aloud); avoiding particularly the hysterical giggler, for the effect depends upon maintaining the atmospheric pressure, and Maeterlinck treads close to the line that separates the sublime from the ridiculous and, as he himself confesses, he occasionally steps over. Read the original if you have any knowledge whatever of French, for the language is of the simplest, and in these veiled dramas a slight additional haziness does no harm. (The French edition is published by Lacomblez, Brussels, in three volumes. Volume I, "La Princesse Maleine", "L'Intruse", "Les Aveugles"; Volume II, "Pelléas et Mélisande", "Alladine et Palomides", "Intérieur", "La mort de Tintagiles"; Volume III, "Aglavaine et Sélysette", "Ariane et Barbe-bleue", "Sœur Beatrice." Volumes I and II, translated by Hovey, are sold by Dodd, Mead and Company in three volumes.) If you are doubtful of your ability to read "the static drama", or of your capacity to enjoy it, begin with "The Interior (The Home)." Here the tragedy is enacted inside the house, while all the talking is done outside. If you find a fascination in it, pass on to "The Intruder" and "The Blind." This last affords unlimited scope to those who are fond of running down symbols. The dead priest in the middle of the group will stand for any form of ecclesiasticism you may have outgrown, and you can give the blind people around him the names of all the philosophers you know, according to the degree of their blindness and their reliance upon rationalism, intuitionalism, child psychology, animal psychology, etc., for a way out. But don't think you have to label them at all if you don't like to.

To understand "The Blue Bird," all you have to do is to become a child. Then after you grow up again you may find that you understand it still better. It was first presented in Russia, where it was played by fifty-two companies. London and New York saw it before Paris, where it was put on the stage for the first time five years after it appeared elsewhere, with Madame Georgette Leblanc in the rôle of Light. (English version, Dodd, Mead and Company.) Maeterlinck has taken out the forest conspiracy because it scared the children, and substituted a new act containing one of his most original characters, the Happiness of Running Barefoot in the Dew, who is apparently a daughter of Doctor Kneipp. Madame Maeterlinck has prepared "The Blue Bird for Children" in story form for schools (Silver, Burdett and Company).

"Mary Magdalene" is played by Olga Nethersole, but may be as well read as seen. "Monna Vanna" was prohibited by the Censor in England until 1914, but was played in this country by Bertha Kalich, without offense. The only play by Maeterlinck that is at all "Frenchy" is one he translated from the English of John Ford. (Dodd, Mead and Company publish "Joyzelle" and "Monna Vanna", "Aglavaine and Sélysette", "Mary Magdalene", "Pelléas and Mélisande", "Princess Maleine", "The Intruder, and Other Plays", and "Sister Beatrice",

MAURICE MAETERLINCK

and "Ariane and Blue Beard." Harper publishes "Monna Vanna"; Crowell published "Pelléas and Mélisande"; R. F. Seymour, Chicago, publishes "Twelve Songs of Maeterlinck." Several of the plays can be found in back numbers of *Poet Lore* sold by R. G. Badger, Boston.)

A comprehensive bibliography will be found in the life of Maeterlinck by Montrose J. Moses (Duffield). We have also in English brief biographies by Gérard Harry (Allen and Sons) and J. Bithel (Scribner). The sketch by William Sharp in the "Warner Library of the World's Best Literature" is remarkable for its insight, and the reader may also be referred to Hunneker's "Iconoclasts", Thorold's "Six Masters of Disillusion", and the article on "Maeterlinck's Philosophy of Life", by Professor John Dewey of Columbia in the *Hibbert Journal*, July, 1911. The lover of Maeterlinck, whose affection is capable of being alienated, should beware of reading the very clever parody on his style in Owen Seaman's "Borrowed Plumes" (Holt).

CHAPTER II

HENRI BERGSON

The history of philosophy shows us chiefly the ceaselessly renewed efforts of reflection laboring to attenuate difficulties, to resolve contradictions, to measure with an increasing approximation a reality incommensurable with our thought. But from time to time bursts forth a soul which seems to triumph over these complications by force of simplicity, the soul of artist or of poet, keeping close to its origin, reconciling with a harmony felt by the heart terms perhaps irreconcilable by the intelligence. The language which it speaks, when it borrows the voice of philosophy, is not similarly understood by everybody. Some think it vague, and so it is in what it expresses. Others feel it precise, because they experience all it suggests. To many ears it brings only the echo of a vanished past, but others hear in it as in a prophetic dream the joyous song of the future.

THESE words, which Bergson used in his eulogy of his teacher, Ravaisson, before the French Academy of Moral and Political Sciences, may be applied with greater appropriateness to Bergson himself. For he, far more than Ravaisson, has shown himself an original force in the world of thought, and his philosophy also appears to some people reactionary

[44]

in tendency and to others far in advance of anything hitherto formulated. But to all it appears important. "Nothing like it since Descartes", they say in France. "Nothing like it since Kant", they say in Germany. His lecture room is the largest in the Collège de France, but it is too small to accommodate the crowd which would hear him. They begin to gather at half-past three for the five o'clock lecture, though they have to listen to a political economist to hold their seats. A cosmopolitan crowd it is that on Wednesdays awaits the lecturer, talking more languages than have ordinarily been heard in the same room at any time during the period from the strike on the Tower of Babel to the universal adoption of Esperanto. French, Italian, English, American, German, Yiddish, and Russian are to be distinguished among them; perhaps the last predominate among the foreign tongues, for young people of both sexes come from Russia in swarms to put themselves under his instruction. This may rouse in us some speculation, even apprehension. Bergsonianism has already assumed some curious forms in the minds of his over-ardent disciples, and what it will become after it has been translated into the Russian language and temperament it would be rash to prophesy.

But the polyglot audience is silent as M. Bergson ascends the rostrum and begins to talk, in slow, smooth, clear tones, accented by nervous gestures of his slender hands. His figure is slight, and his face thin and pointed, almost ecclesiastical in appearance. His hair is slightly gray, but his close-cropped mustache is brown. The eyes are deep, dark, and penetrating, the eyes of seer and scientist together. He lays out his argument in advance in the formal French style, but unlike most French lecturers he does not confine himself to notes. His quick turns of thought break through the conventional forms of logic and find expression in striking and original similes drawn from his wide range of reading. I suppose all professors are given nicknames by their students; at least all who are either loved or hated, and that includes all who amount to anything. Bergson's students call him "the lark", because the higher he flies the sweeter he sings. His voice, indeed, seems to come down from some altitudinous region of the upper atmosphere, so clear and thin and high and penetrating it is. A writer in the *London News* put it very well when he said of Bergson's London lecture, "No one ever spoke before a large audience with more complete self-possession and less self-assertion."

[46]

H Bergson

HENRI BERGSON

As an experienced teacher he appreciates the importance of repetition, and in his lectures brings up the same idea in many varied forms and italicizes with his voice the essential points. All his life he has been a teacher, climbing up the regular educational ladder rung by rung to the top.

Henri Bergson was born in the heart of Paris, the Montmartre quarter, on October 18, 1859. He is descended from a prominent Jewish family of Poland and he owes his excellent command of the English language to his mother, for he always spoke that language with her. At the age of nine he entered the Lycée Condorcet, only a few blocks from his house on the Rue Lamartine. He was a good student and worked hard, particularly on geography, which was most difficult for him. Mathematics was his favorite study, and he then intended to make it his life work, but instead he chose a harder road, for, as he told me, philosophy is much more difficult, requires more concentrated thought than mathematics. Before he left the Lycée at the age of eighteen he won a prize for a solution to a mathematical problem, and the *Annales de Mathématiques* published his paper in full.

Next he entered the École Normale Supérieure, where he came under the influence of Ravaisson,

Lachelier, and Boutroux. On graduation, in 1881, he was made professor of philosophy in the Lycée of Angers for two years, afterward for five years at Clermont, then back to Paris, first in the Collège Rollin and later in the Lycée Henri IV. In 1898 he was promoted to the École Normale Supérieure, and two years later to the Collège de France. In 1901 he was elected to the Institute, and in 1914 to the Academy.

The rapid spread of his philosophy in France is due not only to its intrinsic value and the eloquence with which he presents it, but in part also to his having been a teacher of teachers. By his twenty years' work in the secondary schools or *lycées* of the provinces and Paris, and in the Superior Normal School, he has molded the thought of thousands of young men who are now teaching and writing and ruling in France. His present position as lecturer to miscellaneous audiences in the College of France, though more conspicuous, is really not more influential than his earlier work. He has the faculty of arousing the enthusiasm and personal devotion of his students, so the soil all over the country was prepared in advance for the propagation of his ideas, and now all he has to do is to sow them broadcast. We may observe something of the kind

[48]

in our own country, where Dewey's influence has been largely exercised through personal contact with teachers. If he had never published a line, the colleges, normal and high schools in the western half of the United States would, nevertheless, be teaching anonymous Deweyism. A philosopher who cares more for influence than celebrity will prefer a chair where he can reach the largest number of future teachers to any other position however exalted.

We are not left to speculation as to the extent of Bergson's influence in French education. A questionnaire on the teaching of philosophy in the *lycées* conducted by Binet [1] showed that his ideas were the dominant force of the time. One school reported that "four professors here have adopted them without reserve and made them the soul of their teaching." It is interesting to note that not one of these high school professors mentioned either materialism or pantheism among their various philosophic creeds. They were equally divided between objective and subjective thinkers, or, say, between realists and idealists.

Bergson himself was a materialist to start with, and he worked his way up into his present spiritual-

[1] Reported in the *Bulletin de la Société française de Philosophie*, 1908.

istic philosophy when he found the inadequacy of his early conceptions. His taste was for the exact sciences, and in them he excelled while at school. He intended at that time to devote himself to the study of mechanics, and his youthful ambition was to continue and develop the philosophy of Herbert · Spencer, of whom he was then an enthusiastic admirer.

But as he studied the formulas of mechanics with a view of discovering their philosophical implications, and of utilizing them in the explanation of the universe, he was struck with their inadequacy, even falsity, when applied to the phenomena of life and mind. In particular he was troubled by the symbol t which occurs so frequently in mathematical and physical formulas, and is supposed to stand for "time." It is represented geometrically by a straight line just like the three dimensions of space. In fact, as Bergson points out, "time" as used in physical science is nothing more or less than a fourth dimension of space. It is purely a spatial conception, an empty framework in which events may be arranged in order as objects are set up in a row on a shelf. There is no change or development in it, for past and future are all the same to it.

Now, when Bergson compared this physical conception of "time" with real time or duration as he felt it within himself, he found they were entirely different things. For the mind the past does not stretch out in a line behind. It is rolled up into the present and projected toward the future. Still less is there a path or several optional paths definitely laid out ahead of us in the future. We break our own paths as we go forward. It is like the big snowballs that we boys used to roll up to make forts out of; all the snow it has passed over is a part of it, and in front the snow is trackless.

The mechanical formulas of science are admirably adapted to the purpose for which they were designed, that is, the handling of matter, but they are misleading as applied to living beings, and especially to the human mind, which is the farthest removed from the realm of material mechanics. Here is true freedom and initiative.

The advocate of free will always gets beaten in the argument with the determinist when he meets him on his own ground, for adopting the spatial conception of time and the dynamic conception of motives, reduces man to a machine and, of course, makes him amenable to the ordinary laws of mechanics. If it is correct to represent the future as two crossroads in front of the undecided individual and he pulled to right and left by "motives" on either side, then the determinist has it all his own way. The case has been conceded to him in advance, and the libertarian can only flinch from his logic. But Bergson holds that when the determinist pretends to talk about the future, he really is regarding it as already past, as definitely mapped and virtually existent.

As Bergson's first book, "Time and Free Will", was devoted to the overthrow of the metaphysical argument for determinism, so his second, "Matter and Memory", was devoted to the overthrow of the psychological argument, which is that the mind and the brain are merely different aspects of the same thing (monism) or that their action is parallel so that a certain state of consciousness always corresponds to a certain molecular motion (dualism). Since the activities of the brain are presumably controlled by the physical and chemical laws, then must be also the mental activities identical or inseparably connected with them. But Bergson, taking the position of an extreme dualist, argues that the mind is distinct from matter and only in part dependent upon it, that memories are not altogether stored in the brain or anywhere in space, and that the brain is essentially nothing more than an instrument of action.

HENRI BERGSON

The same is true of our senses, of our bodily organism in general. They are made for practical, not speculative, purposes. The things nearest to us are seen largest and clearest. The eye is useful because its vision is limited. If it were susceptible to all rays, like our skin, we should get, not vision, but sunburn. Now the understanding, also having a pragmatic origin, limits our knowledge just as the eye limits our vision, and for the same purpose.

Let me give a few examples of this limitation of our senses and of our intellect. Suppose we are looking at a horse or automobile going past in the street. We get an immediate sense of the movement very decidedly, but the motion itself we cannot see. We must first analyze the motion; that is, take it apart, break it up into something that is not motion. This we can do with a kinetoscope camera which takes snapshots at the rate of fifty a second. These successive pictures do not give the motion, no matter how rapidly they are taken. Each represents the object standing still, or if not quick enough for that, the picture is blurred; but show these still-life photographs to us in quick succession, and we no longer perceive them as separate views but as continuous motion. Why can the camera so deceive us? Simply because our eyes work in the same way. They are cameras, and the exposure time of the retina is about the same as that of the moving picture films. A moving object looked at steadily is merely a blurred band. But if we wink rapidly, we can catch glimpses of the legs of the horse or the spokes of the wheel, thus like the kinetoscope transforming motion into immobility by intermittent attention.

Look closely at a portrait in this book, and you will see that it consists of pure black and white. Needless to say that the face portrayed was not composed of black spots of various sizes on a white ground. In the original there were no black, no white, and no dots. There were only even shadings, lighter and darker. The picture is an absolute misrepresentation. Yet viewed with the naked eye at sufficient distance to put the dots out of sight, it imitates the shading of the original well enough to be called a "half-tone plate", although there is really not a half tone in it, nothing but black and white.

Now this trick of decomposing continuous motion into successive pictures like the kinetoscope and decomposing continuous space into successive spots like the printing process, is the way we do our thinking. The mind goes by jerks like the eye. When we think of the course of history we break it up into blocks of handy size, comparing century with century, year with year. This is perfectly justifiable, very useful, in fact inevitable, and quite innocent, provided we realize that it is a logical fiction, adapted to practical purposes merely. The trouble has come from not recognizing this. People generally, and especially scientists and philosophers, have been inclined to regard this process of rationali- zation as the way of getting at reality, instead of as a mere tool for handling reality.

Long ago, when men first began to think hard, they discovered the inadequacy of mere thinking. Zeno of Elea propounded among other puzzles that of Achilles and the tortoise, which has kept the world guessing for twenty-four centuries. While Achilles is making up his handicap, the tortoise has gone on a bit farther, and when Achilles has covered this distance, the tortoise is not there, but still ahead, and since space is conceived as infinitely divisible, Achilles would take an infinity of time to catch up. I do not suppose the experiment was ever tried. That was not the way of the Greeks. They placed too much reliance upon their brains and too little on anything outside of them to put a theory to the test of experiment. But it has been agreed everywhere, always and by all, that Achilles would catch the tortoise, and a considerable proportion of each generation have tried to explain how he could, often succeeding to their own satisfaction, but rarely to the satisfaction of other people. For the point to this puzzle is not to get the answer, but to say why it puzzles us, and to this point philosophers from Aristotle to Bergson have devoted much study; and doubtless the end is not yet.

I remember well the day when that ancient jest was first sprung upon me in the University of Kansas, by the instructor in philosophy, a bright young man just on from Harvard, who had the Eleatics at his finger tips. Several of the boys volunteered to explain it, but I, having the longest arm and snappiest fingers, got the floor. I suggested that we substitute a greyhound chasing a jack rabbit for Achilles and the tortoise, who must be tired of running so long. Both greyhound and jack rabbit progress by jumps, and I argued, with the aid of a piece of chalk, that these could be measured and laid off on the prairie, here represented by the blackboard, and so the whole thing figured out. But the instructor denied my petition for a change of venue. He stuck to Greece and refused to meet me on my native soil, so I retired discomfited. I thought him unaccommodating at the time, but I see now that he was merely wise. Wariness is often so mistaken for disobligingness. The paradox is solved by science and by common sense by assuming that Achilles and the tortoise move by jumps instead of continuously and then comparing these jumps, for they are of finite length and number.

In short, we know what motion is by common sense, by feeling, by intuition, but when we come to reason about it, and especially when we come to talk about it, we have to substitute for it something that is not motion, but is easier to handle and near enough like it, so that ordinarily it serves just as well. It is as much like it as the short, straight lines, substituted by the mathematician, are like the segments of the curve he is trying to solve. What is true of motion is true in a way of all our definitions, formulations, laws, and categories; they are not the real things, but merely handy surrogates. They represent some particular phase of reality more or less satisfactorily. These formulas are not designed to pick all the locks of Nature's treasure chests. They are good for the lock they are designed for and sometimes others, not all. The master key to all locks either does not exist or is too cumbrous to be wielded by man.

Bergson's theory of personality arises naturally

out of his conception of time. Time is said to have one dimension. Yes, if we symbolize it by a line; otherwise not, it has no dimension. The impersonal time of the philosophers and scientists is merely the spatial symbol of duration. What our experience shows us is not this empty artificial uneventful time, but *duration*. And not merely duration, but *durations*, for there are as many durations of different interval rhythm as there are consciousnesses. This is what is real in time. Time is really the continuous unrolling of our conscious life, of psychologic states which do not become distinct except when it pleases us to divide them. Personality is a continuity of *indivisible movement*. We can draw a bucket of water out of the river, and then another bucketful, but we can never get the stream in this way, for the stream is essentially movement. The movement is what is substantial about the stream.

From immobile states we can never make of life what experience actually gives us, for life is change. Only by seizing this change directly in an integral experience can we solve the problem. To true realities no concept is applicable. Reality must be regarded itself, in itself, just as it is; and in giving a description of it, we can fix only the image of it before our eyes.

HENRI BERGSON

The guiding thread of philosophical problems is that the intellect is an instrument of action which has developed itself in the course of centuries in order to triumph over the difficulties that matter opposes to life. The intellect has constituted itself for the purpose of a battle. The obstacles which it would overthrow are those of brute matter. The categories of the understanding are constructed with a view of action upon matter. So where our intellect seeks to know something else than the material world, it finds itself unable to grasp it. The whole history of the evolution of life combines to show that intelligence is an instrumental function for action upon matter, to formulate and present the laws which permit us to foresee, and therefore to forestall.

In dealing with a reality like personality, the intellect will first attempt to handle the subject with the same processes that it employs for inert matter, therefore it ends in a logical *impasse*. This is the origin of the difficulties of the question. The concepts which it would apply to personality are made only for the material world. We do not know how to apply them adequately to the life of the mind, which overflows them.

To direct our attention upon the stream of our

consciousness breaks it up and immobilizes it. But it may be reached by another kind of introspection, which consists in letting live, in trying to reënforce vitality. In this way activity may become consciousness without ceasing to be active. Thus the ego may be seized as it really is, as a transition and a continuity.

In his theory of evolution Bergson draws a sharp distinction between intelligence and instinct. As intelligence has reached its highest point in the human race, so instinct has reached its highest point in the ants, bees, and wasps. Here we see instinct attaining its ends by the employment of the most varied and complicated expedients. The ant is lord of the subsoil as man is lord of the soil. The solitary wasps, whom Maeterlinck would despise as primitive individualists in comparison with the socialized bees, are used by Bergson to illustrate his theory of instinct. These insects provide for the future needs of their larvæ by storing up in their underground nest spiders, beetles, or caterpillars. These are to be kept alive, as we keep turtles and lobsters, so they will be fresh, and in order to prevent them from escaping, the wasp paralyzes them by stinging them at the point or points where the motor nerves meet. One species of wasp pierces the ganglia of its caterpillar by nine successive thrusts of its sting and then squeezes the head in its mandibles, enough to cause paralysis without death. Other kinds of wasps have to use other forms of surgical treatment, according to the kind of insect they put into storage. How can this be explained? If we call it intelligence, we must assume that the wasp or its ancestors has been endowed with a knowledge of insect anatomy such as we hesitate to credit to any being lower in the scale of life than a professor of entomology. If we adopt a mechanistic hypothesis, we must assume that this marvelous skill in surgery has been gradually acquired in the course of thousands of generations, either by the survival of the descendants of those insects who happened to have stuck their stings into the nine right places (Darwinism), or by the inheritance of the acquired habit of stinging a certain species of caterpillar in that particular way (Lamarckianism). But since this knowledge or skill is never of use to the individual insect and is of no use to the species until it has arrived at a considerable degree of perfection, we can hardly adopt either theory without straining our imagination.

But the assumed difficulties vanish if we adopt the Bergsonian point of view and regard the caterpillar and wasp as two parts of the same process. It is no wonder then that they are fitted together. Slayer and slain have developed for that purpose, and what is apparently antagonism is really coöperation. The importance of this theory to those who are troubled about the moral interpretation of the universe is obvious, for the stinging of the caterpillar would seem something like picking a sliver out of the left hand by the right, but Bergson does not go into this question at all.

The formation of the eye, which is the source of much perplexity to evolutionists of all schools, provides Bergson with an excellent illustration of his theory. The eye of mollusks is similar in form and identical in function with the eye of the vertebrates, yet the two are composed of different elements and grow in a different way. The retina of the vertebrate is produced by an expansion of the central nervous system of the young embryo. It is, so to speak, a part of the brain coming out to see. In the mollusk, on the contrary, the retina is formed from the external layer of the embryo. Here heredity is out of the question because of this difference of formation and because the man is not descended from the mollusk nor the mollusk from man. The structure of the eye involves the combination of such a large number of elements and must satisfy so many conditions before it is good for anything, that it is practically impossible to explain it either as the effect of the action of light or as the result of an accretion of slight accidental variations.

But Bergson, coming in with his philosophic faith at the point where science leaves off, calls attention to the fact that while the eye is a complicated structure, seeing is one simple act. Why not begin our explanation with the simple, instead of the complex? The analytical method of the intellect, though useful in its place, does not lead us to the meaning of reality. It is as if we could only see a picture as broken up into a mosaic, or as if we could only consider a movement of the hand in the mathematician's way, as an infinite series of points arranged in a curve.

So the eye with its marvelous complexity of structure, may be only the simple act of vision, divided *for us* into a mosaic of cells, whose order seems marvelous to us because we have conceived the whole as an assemblage. . . .

Mechanism and finalism both go too far, for they attribute to Nature the most formidable of the labors of Hercules in holding that she has exalted to the simple act of vision an infinity of infinitely complex elements, whereas Nature has had no more trouble

in making an eye than I have in lifting my hand.
Nature's simple act has divided itself automatically
into an infinity of elements which are then found
to be coördinated to one idea, just as the movement
of my hand has dropped an infinity of points which
are then found to satisfy one equation. — "Creative
Evolution", pp. 90–91.

Bergson seems born to be an exception to Amiel's
criticism of French philosophy: "The French lack
that intuitive faculty to which the living unity of
things is revealed." "Their logic never goes beyond
the category of mechanism nor their metaphysic
beyond dualism."

M. Bergson's residence is the Villa Montmorency
in Auteuil, a quiet quarter of Paris, lying between
the Seine and the Bois de Boulogne. In summer
he goes to Switzerland for greater seclusion and the
stimulus of a higher altitude upon his thought.
Here I had the pleasure of spending an afternoon
with him. From Geneva, where I was staying, I
took the railroad that skirts the lake upon the western side to Nyon, an old Roman town at the foot
of the Dole, the highest peak of the Swiss Jura.
St. Cergue, my destination, was nine miles inland
and a half a mile up. The distance I had to go was
therefore the square root of the sum of the squares of
these distances, but I did not figure it out, because,

according to Bergson, we live in time rather than space, and duration is not a measure of length. So I can only say that it was one of the longest and pleasantest hypotenuses I ever traversed. For there was a sense of exhilaration in rising ever higher as the carriage zigzagged through the woods, and in getting a grander view each time we stopped at a turn to give way to an automobile chugging slowly up or coasting swiftly down. Arrived at the little village of St. Cergue, I had still a climb and a search among the hotels, pensions, and summer homes scattered over the mountainside for Villa Bois-gentil. This was found in the middle of a meadow backed by a forest of firs, a square, two-story house, simply furnished but with no affectation of rusticity, as is common in American country homes. From the inclosed porch there is a glorious view of Mont Blanc, with the long blue crescent of Lake Geneva curving around the ramparts of its base. But, as with many another Swiss view, the effect is marred by the presence of a big box of a hotel in the immediate foreground.

One would have thought from the cordiality of my reception that a philosopher had nothing better to do than to entertain a wandering American journalist. At lunch I had an opportunity of meeting also Madame and Mademoiselle Bergson, and afterward a long talk with Professor Bergson, who later accompanied me down the steep mountain path to the village and along the winding road through the woods. His conversation has the charm of his books, the enthusiasm for the mission of philosophy, the wealth of illustrations drawn from many fields of science and art, the freshness and inspiration of his novel point of view, the candidness in the consideration of opposing arguments, the unaffected, unpretentious manner, the absence of the professional jealousy and personal arrogance which has been characteristic of many original thinkers. The reader will notice that in his reviews and criticisms of the historic systems of philosophy, he never seeks to overthrow them, but is always trying to see how much of them he can save and assimilate. He believes that it is possible for metaphysics to have a continuous and positive development like the natural sciences, each man building on what has gone before, instead of setting up a new school and endeavoring to secure a personal following.[1]

I took the liberty of extending to Professor Berg-

[1] For his views on the possibility of scientific metaphysics, see *Le Parallélisme psycho-physique et la métaphysique positive* in *Bulletin de la Société française de Philosophie*, June, 1901; and *Introduction à la métaphysique* in *Revue de Métaphysique et de Morale*, January, 1903.

son an invitation to America, for I was able to assure him of a hearty welcome on account of the deep interest already taken here in his thought. The work of James and Dewey prepared the way for Bergson in this country, for his philosophy may be regarded as a constructive system built upon pragmatic criticism. Indeed, he has been accused by his opponents of stealing Yankee psychology and making metaphysics out of it. The truth is, James and Bergson pursued through many years lines of thought of similar tendency but of independent development, though each has repeatedly taken occasion to express his appreciation of the work of the other. It is a case of psycho-metaphysical parallelism rather than of interaction.

In February, 1913, Professor Bergson came to America at the invitation of Columbia University and gave two series of lectures, one in French and the other in English, on *Spiritualité et Liberté* and the Method of Philosophy. One would find reason to question the common assertion that nowadays no interest is taken in metaphysical problems when he saw the lecture rooms packed with people from the city as well as students from all departments of the university. A line of automobiles stood waiting along Broadway, as the litters waited in the streets of Rome when Plotinus, the Neoplatonist, came to lecture there seventeen hundred years ago. Those who could not beg, buy, or borrow a ticket of admission formed a line outside the door, hoping that some who had tickets would fail to appear, but that did not often happen. A lunette was discovered over the door which commanded the lecture room, and here gathered a compact group of the excluded, finding room for one eye or one ear apiece, but the fainting of a lady in the crush put a stop to this privilege. In the downtown department stores Bergson's books were stacked up on the "best sellers" counter. His American publisher sold in two years half as many copies of "Creative Evolution" as had been sold in France in fifteen. Yet Bergson is a prophet not without honor in his own country. The three weeks he spent here were so crowded with engagements that he had to be kept running on a schedule as close as a railroad time-table. As he was leaving, I asked Professor Bergson the banal question of what he thought of America. He answered: "I shall always remember America as the Land of Interrupted Conversations. I have met so many interesting people with whom I should like to talk, but then somebody else equally interesting comes up."

HENRI BERGSON

M. Bergson believes that it is possible to make any philosophical idea clear and acceptable to the multitude. In this he obviously differs from other philosophers, many of whom do not think it possible and some of whom do not think it desirable. But to gain the wider audience, the author must take great pains with his style. The fault with translations is that the swing, the rhythm, is apt to be lost or altered, and this is essential to the impression as well as the right words. I spoke to him of the difficulty of finding an exact English equivalent of *élan vital*, which is the key word of his "Evolution créatrice", and he replied that he thought that "impetus", the word chosen by Dr. Arthur Mitchell in his translation of the work, was better than any of the others which had been suggested, such as "impulse", "momentum", "movement", "onrush", "push", "force", and "urge."

.M. Bergson's method of composition is based on his theory of style. In undertaking a new book he spends as many years as may be necessary to the mastery of the literature of the subject and the development of his ideas. Then when he starts in to compose, he sets aside all his books and notes, and writes at a furious rate so as to get the book down as nearly as possible in the form it took in his mind at one time, jotting down his thoughts as rapidly as they come, often in fragmentary sentences and words, so as not to interrupt the movement of his mind. Then having put on paper the essentials of his theme with its original impetus, he devotes himself to the long process of revision, verification, and correction.

To art in all its forms Bergson has given a large place in his philosophy. The little book in which he has touched upon it, "Le Rire" (Laughter), is not so much of a digression from his fundamental line of thought as may appear. He explains that ridicule has developed as a method of social control, to whip people into line, to punish them for willful or absent-minded disregard of social usages. Laughter is incompatible with emotion. The comic addresses itself to pure intelligence. A joke cannot be perceived until the heart has a momentary anæsthesia. There is nothing comic except human beings. Man has been defined as "the laughing animal." He is also the only laughable animal. Man becomes ridiculous when we regard him from an intellectualist standpoint; that is, as a machine. The attitudes, gestures, and movements of the human body are laughable in the exact degree that they seem to us mechanical. We always laugh when persons seem like things.

The bearing of this theory of the ridiculous upon his philosophy is so obvious that he does not need to state it. Bergson, too, might use ridicule as a weapon and laugh determinism out of court. The man of the mechanists would be as funny as a jack-in-the-box.

In the same volume he gives his view of the function of art, from which a few sentences may be quoted here:

What is the object of art? If reality struck our senses and our consciousness directly; if we could enter into immediate communication with things and with each other, I believe that art would be useless, or rather that we would all be artists, for our souls would then vibrate continuously in unison with nature. Our eyes, aided by our memory, would cut out in space and fix in time inimitable pictures. Our glance would seize in passing, sculptured in the living marble of the human body, bits of statuary as beautiful as those of antiquity. We would hear singing in the depths of our souls like music, sometimes gay, more often plaintive, always original, the uninterrupted melody of our interior life. All this is around us, all this is in us, and yet nothing of all this is perceived by us distinctly. Between nature and us — what do I say? — between us and our own consciousness, a veil interposes, a thick veil for the common man, a thin veil, almost transparent, for the artist and the poet. What fairy has woven this veil ? Was it through malice or through friendliness ? It is necessary to live, and life requires that we apprehend things relatively to our needs. Living consists in acting. To live is to receive from objects only the *useful* impression in order to respond to it by the appropriate reactions; the other impressions must obliterate themselves or come to us only confusedly. I look and I believe I see, I listen and believe I hear, I study myself and I believe I read to the bottom of my heart. But what I see and what I hear from the external world is simply what my senses extract from it in order to throw light upon my conduct; what I know of myself is what flows on the surface, what takes part in action. My senses and my consciousness give me only a practical simplification of reality.

Thus, whether it be painting, sculpture, poetry or music, art has no other object than to dissipate the practically useful symbols, the generalities conventionally and socially accepted, in short all that masks reality for us, in order to bring us face to face with reality itself. It is a misunderstanding on this point that has given rise to the debate between realism and idealism in art. Art is certainly only a more direct vision of reality. But this purity of perception implies a rupture with useful convention, an innate and specially localized disinterestedness of the sense or of the consciousness, in short, a certain immateriality of life which is what has always been called idealism. So one might say without in the least playing upon the sense of the words, that realism is in the work when idealism is in the soul, and that it is by force of ideality alone that one can regain contact with reality.

HENRI BERGSON

There are various other ways besides art whereby we may recover and strengthen the faculty of intuition, which has been suffered to atrophy through too exclusive a reliance upon rational processes. There is, for example, action, life itself, the sense of living, which brings us into immediate contact with reality. By the help of science, art, and philosophy, we may achieve sympathy, a feeling of the kinship of nature, a consciousness of interpenetration, a realization of the meaning of evolution. Above all, philosophy has this aim and power, to develop another faculty, complementary to the intellect, that will open to us a perspective on the other half of reality, not capable of being confined in the rigid formulas of deductive logic.

There are things that intelligence alone is able to seek but which, by itself, it will never find. These things instinct alone can find, but it will never seek them.

Intelligence and instinct are turned in opposite directions, the former toward inert matter, the latter toward life. Intelligence by means of science, which is its work, will deliver up to us more and more completely the secret of physical operations; of life it brings us, and moreover only claims to bring us, a translation in terms of inertia. It goes all around life, taking from the outside the greatest possible number of views of it, drawing it into itself instead of entering into it. But it is to the very inwardness of life that *intuition* leads — by intuition I mean instinct that has become disinterested, self-conscious, capable of reflecting upon its object and of enlarging it indefinitely.

We see that the intellect, so skillful in dealing with the inert, is awkward the moment it touches the living. Whether it wants to treat the life of the body or the life of the mind, it proceeds with the rigor, the stiffness, and the brutality of an instrument not designed for such use. The history of hygiene or of pedagogy teaches us much in this matter.

In Bergson's system metaphysics occupies the same place that it does in the works of Aristotle. Metaphysics is simply what is beyond physics, not something antagonistic to it. He has not, like many modern philosophers, been contemptuous toward physiological psychology. On the contrary, he has mastered it and built upon it. This is the reason, I think, why his ideas have met with such swift acceptance. It is as absurd for a philosopher nowadays to attempt to confine himself to the data accessible to Plato as it would be for a mathematician to attempt to solve the problems of modern physics with the use of the methods of Euclid.

Bergson applied his theory of the relation of mind and brain to the explanation of the mechanism of dreaming, in an address before the *Institut psy-*

chologique on March 28, 1901.[1] Here he showed how the obscure sensations of sight, touch, and hearing which reach us even during sleep furnish the basis for our dreams, and how our memories fit into this framework, so the process is similar to that of ordinary perception except that the critical faculty is less vigilant than in a waking state. Thus, light flashing upon the closed eyes may give :ise to a dream of fire, and the recumbent posture and consequent absence of pressure on the soles of the feet give us the idea of floating in the air. The following passage from this paper on dreams is of especial interest, for in it Bergson brings forward the theory which since then Freud and his school have developed and in many cases carried to extravagant lengths, — the theory that our memories are stored in a state of tension like steam in a boiler, and may rise into consciousness in various guises when the vigilance of the individual is relaxed :

Our memories, at any given moment, form a solid whole, a pyramid, so to speak, whose point is inserted precisely into our present action. But behind the memories which are concerned in our occupations and are revealed by means of it, there are others, thousands of others, stored below the scene illumi-

[1] Published in the *Revue scientifique*, June 8, 1901, and in English in *The Independent*, October 23–30, 1913, and in book form, 1914.

nated by consciousness. Yes, I believe indeed that all our past life is there, preserved even to the most infinitesimal details, and that we forget nothing, and that all that we have felt, perceived, thought, willed, from the first awakening of our consciousness, survives indestructibly. But the memories which are preserved in these obscure depths are there in the state of invisible phantoms. They aspire, perhaps, to the light, but they do not even try to rise to it; they know that it is impossible and that I, as a living and acting being, have something else to do than to occupy myself with them.

But suppose that, at a given moment, I become *disinterested* in the present situation, in the present action — in short, in all which previously has fixed and guided my memory; suppose, in other words, that I am asleep. Then these memories, perceiving that I have taken away the obstacle, have raised the trapdoor which has kept them beneath the floor of consciousness, arise from the depths; they rise, they move, they perform in the night of unconsciousness a great dance macabre. They rush together to the door which has been left ajar. They all want to get through. But they cannot; there are too many of them. From the multitudes which are called, which will be chosen? It is not hard to say. Formerly, when I was awake, the memories which forced their way were those which could involve claims of relationship with the present situation, with what I saw and heard around me. Now it is more vague images which occupy my sight, more indecisive sounds which affect my ear, more indistinct touches which are distributed over the surface of my body, but there are also the more numerous sensations which arise from the deepest parts of the organism. So, then, among the phantom memories which aspire to fill themselves with color, with sonority, in short with materiality, the only ones that succeed are those which can assimilate themselves with the color-dust that we perceive, the external and internal sensations that we catch, etc., and which, besides, respond to the effective tone of our general sensibility. When this union is effected between the memory and the sensation, we have a dream.

Bergson may be called a man of three books, if we ignore "Laughter", which is merely a flying buttress of his system. In the first, known in English as "Time and Free Will", he develops his theory of vital duration as distinct from physical time, which has been the guiding clew of all his later thinking. This volume, completed in 1887, was the outcome of a four years' study of the physical, psychological, and metaphysical conceptions of time and space. For the second book, dealing with the relation of the mind to the brain, it was necessary to master the voluminous literature of the subject, especially the clinical and experimental researches on aphasia and localization of function. This required nine years of study, embodied in "Matter and Memory", appearing in 1896. In the preparation for the third book he devoted eleven years to the study of biology and produced "Creative Evolution" in 1907. According to this rate of increase, we might expect his fourth volume in 1923, but it would be obviously unfair to apply to M. Bergson himself the mathematical determinism that he repudiates.

I call attention to this preliminary study of the sciences, because there is a danger that the anti-intellectualist tendency of the pragmatic movement should lead to a disregard of the importance of scientific research. That this danger is real and present, was shown in the Binet report on the teaching of philosophy, previously referred to. Some of the professors complained that their students, under the influence of Bergson's ideas, had come to have a disdain for the tedious and laborious methods of experimental science, believing that science does not give us reality, and assuming that, while science is good enough for mechanics and physicians, it is indifferent to philosophers.

When this point was brought up for discussion in the *Société française de Philosophie*, M. Bergson made an indignant reply, declaring that in the theories attributed to him he recognized nothing that he had taught or written. He had never contemned science or subordinated it to metaphysics.

Mathematics, for instance, what have I said of that ? That, however great may be the part played in it by the creative imagination, it must not lose sight of space and matter; that matter and space are realities; that matter is weighted with geometry; that geometry is consequently not a mere play but a true point of contact with the absolute. I attribute the same absolute value to the physical sciences. It is true they enunciate laws of which the form would have been different if other variables, other units of measure, had been chosen, and especially if the problems had been propounded chronologically in a different order. But all this is because we are obliged to break up nature and to examine one by one the problems it sets for us. Really, physics strives for the absolute, and it approaches more and more as it advances this ideal limit. I should like to know if there exists, among modern conceptions of science, a theory that puts a higher value upon positive science. Most of them give us science as entirely relative to human intelligence. I hold, on the contrary, that it is reality itself, absolute reality, which the mathematical and physical sciences tend to reveal to us. Science only begins to become relative, or rather symbolic, when it approaches from the physico-chemical side, the problems of life and consciousness. But even here it is quite legitimate. It only needs then to be completed by a study of another kind, that is, metaphysics. In short, all my researches have had no other object than to bring about a *rapprochement* between metaphysics and science and to consolidate the one with the other without sacrificing anything of either, after having first clearly distinguished the one from the other.

This outspoken and emphatic language ought to clear the air of many current misconceptions of

Bergson's philosophy. Now that he has laid down his fundamental principles, it is to be hoped that he will next take up their applications to the interpretation of history and the problems of conduct. If he does not do this himself, others will do it for him, and doubtless not always in accordance with his intentions. In fact, they are already doing it. In France, Bergsonianism is not an academic speculation, but an active force in some of the most important movements of the day. We hear of a Bergsonian art and a Bergsonian literature as well as a Bergsonian Catholicism and a Bergsonian labor movement. The two last mentioned are of especial interest as showing the influence of his novel views upon the most diverse minds. Just as there were Hegelians of the Right and Hegelians of the Left, so now there are two wings of Bergsonianism, the conservative being the Modernists and the radical being the Syndicalists.

There has rarely been seen such an outburst of enthusiasm for metaphysical thought as that of the French neo-Catholics. The pragmatic philosophy, particularly James's "Varieties of Religious Experience", pointed the way to a new Christian apologetic based upon living experience, instead of abstract reasoning. The young Catholics turned their attention to the saints rather than to the theologians, and found inspiration in a fresh study of the Catholic mystics. In a conception of truth as a growth, as an ideal convergence of beneficial beliefs, rather than as a static limit, and in a conception of history as a progressive process of verification, they attained a point of view which enabled them to retain their ecclesiastical heritage and at the same time to accept the bounty of modern science. But such speculations were deemed dangerous by the Vatican, and the movement was crushed, so far as a movement of such vigor and vitality can be crushed, by the Encyclical and Syllabus issued by Pius X in 1907, and the anti-modernist oath that was later imposed.[1] This was followed in 1914 by the placing of Bergson's works upon the Index of Prohibited Books which no good Catholic may read without the express permission of his spiritual adviser.

At the opposite extreme we find the trades unions or syndicates, whose power has been often demon-

[1] Articles on pragmatic Catholicism may be found in almost any volume of the *Revue Philosophique* and the *Revue de Métaphysique et de Morale* during the first twelve years of the twentieth century. See especially those by Edouard Le Roy, a disciple of James and Bergson. A brief account of the movement is contained in Lalande's "Philosophy in France, 1907", *Philosophical Review*, May, 1908.

strated in recent years, but whose aims and ideals are yet indeterminate and vague. So far it is Will and not Idea that is manifested in the revolutionary labor movement, to use the Schopenhaurian terms. But becoming conscious of the need of a philosophical justification, they have seized upon one side of Bergson's doctrine and declared the *élan ouvrier* brother to the *élan vital*, or a part of it. Their flamboyant phraseology reminds one of 1793 : "The Collège de France collaborates with the Bourse du Travail" and "The flute of personal meditation harmonizes with the trumpets of the social revolution." The syndicalists, like the modernists, have their revolt against dogma, against the catchwords of republicanism as well as against the rigid formulas of Marxianism, against all attempts to confine the future in the past and to impose determinism upon conduct. And when it comes to the enforcement of conformity — or, rather, of uniformity — of profession, there is not much difference between Pope and party.[1]

It is unnecessary to say that M. Bergson teaches neither Catholicism nor revolution, and that he

[1] As representatives of the pragmatic syndicalists may be mentioned George Sorel and Edouard Berth. For an account of the philosophical side of the movement, see *Syndicalistes et Bergsoniens* by C. Bouglé in *Revue du Mois*, April, 1909.

cannot be held accountable for all the various applications of his ideas to practical life. I mention these extremes only to show the range of their actual influence. Whatever may be the fate of Bergson's philosophy, we may be sure it will not leave the world as it found it. It is a force to be reckoned with at all events in the field of action as well as in the realm of pure reason.

Very few references to disputed questions in religion, sociology, and ethics can be found in his works, and since he prefers to use a new, clean, and unconventional vocabulary, he cannot be pocketed in any of the pigeonholes provided in advance by the historians of philosophy. To the demand for a brief formulation of his philosophy, an indignant Bergsonian retorts: "Can you put Maeterlinck's 'Pelléas and Mélisande' into a formula?"

The Post Impressionists and Futurists are fond of ascribing their novel ideas of art to Bergson, but he is not eager to assume the responsibility. When I asked him about it, he said that he had never yet been able to discover his philosophy in their paintings, and further that he was always skeptical of a movement where the theory ran so far ahead of the practice.

It is obvious that the adoption of the pragmatic

principle, particularly in the extreme Bergsonian form, would radically alter our view of the past, and compel a rewriting or at least a rereading of history. If history never repeats itself, what is its lesson for us? Certainly it is not competent to foretell our future, still less to prescribe our actions. The best expression of what seems to me the legitimate ethical deductions of Bergson's philosophy is to be found in the brilliant essays by L. P. Jacks. According to the editor of the *Hibbert Journal*, the highest morality consists, not in following the established rules, but in a voluntary rise into a higher level. The true moral act is original, creative, unprecedented. What would the author of "Folkways", for whom conformity was the only morality, have said to the following:

"Had men all along restricted themselves to the performance of those actions for which the warrant of moral science was then and there available, many crimes perhaps would not have been committed, but it is doubtful if the world would contain the record of a single noble deed. We cannot remind ourselves too often that the most complete scientific knowledge of what has been done up to date will never enable us to answer the question, 'What ought to be done next?'

HENRI BERGSON

"The subject matter of science and the subject matter of morality are entirely different and in a sense opposed; the first is the deed-as-done, the second is the doing of a deed-to-be.

"Conscience rightly understood is no faculty of abstract judgment laying down propositions as to what ought and ought not to be done; it is not a 'voice', though we often name it such, bidding us do this or that; it is rather an *élan vital*, an impulse, an active principle, nay, the good *Will* itself." — "Alchemy of Thought", by L. P. Jacks, pp. 260, 287.

Among the numerous followers of Bergson, none is more enthusiastic or sympathetic than Edouard Le Roy, a modernist Catholic — if that, since the encyclical, is not a contradiction in terms — who has for many years been in close touch with Bergson, and has been especially interested in the religious and ethical applications of his theories. His introduction to Bergson's philosophy is therefore useful, not merely because it gives in brief a competent exposition of Bergson's ideas, for the beginner would probably find it quite as profitable and enjoyable to read the same number of pages of "Creative Evolution", but chiefly because M. Le Roy is in a way an authorized spokesman, and so we can get some notion of Bergson's opinions about questions

[85]

on which he has not yet expressed himself. For example, Bergson in all his books never deals with religion, although it is obvious that his philosophy has the closest relation with religion in many of its aspects. Le Roy, however, is not so reticent, and he closes the volume with the following noteworthy passage :

" In the depths of ourselves we find liberty ; in the depths of universal being we find a demand for creation. Since evolution is creative, each of its moments works for the production of an indeducible and transcendent future. This future must not be regarded as a simple development of the present, a simple expression of germs already given. Consequently we have no authority for saying that there is forever only one order of life, only one plane of action, only one rhythm of duration, only one perspective of existence. And if disconnections and abrupt leaps are visible in the economy of the past — from matter to life, from the animal to man — we have no authority again for claiming that we cannot observe to-day something analogous in the very essence of human life, that the point of view of the flesh, and the point of view of the spirit, the point of view of reason, and the point of view of charity are a homogeneous extension of it. And apart from that, taking life in its first tendency, and in the general direction of its current, it is ascent, growth, upward effort, and a work of spiritualizing and emancipating creation : by that we might define Good, for Good is a path rather than a thing.

"But life may fail, halt, or travel downward. . . . Each species, each individual, each function tends to take itself as its end; mechanism, habit, body and letter, which are, strictly speaking, pure instruments, actually become principles of death. Thus it comes about that life is exhausted in efforts toward self-preservation, allows itself to be converted by matter into captive eddies, sometimes even abandons itself to the inertia of the weight which it ought to raise, and surrenders to the downward current which constitutes the essence of materiality: it is thus that Evil would be defined, as the direction of travel opposed to Good. Now, with man, thought, reflection, and clear consciousness appear. At the same time also properly moral qualifications appear; good becomes duty, evil becomes sin. At this precise moment, a new problem begins, demanding the soundings of a new intuition, yet connected at clear and visible points with previous problems.

"This is the philosophy which some are pleased to say is closed by nature to all problems of a certain order, problems of reason or problems of morality. There is no doctrine, on the contrary, which is more open, and none which, in actual fact, lends itself better to further extension."

I have quoted this entire, because Professor Bergson has given it his indorsement in the plainest terms. In a letter.to M. Le Roy about the book, he says :

Your study could not be more conscientious or true to the original. Nowhere is this sympathy more in evidence than where you point the possibilities of further developments of the doctrine. In this direction I should myself say exactly what you have said.

The passage quoted above from M. Le Roy's book has, then, almost the significance of a signed statement. It was observed that in his lectures in New York Professor Bergson was much more outspoken than formerly in his views upon religious matters; as, for example, when he replied affirmatively to the question whether he believed in immortality or not. It may be anticipated that his future work will be in the development of his philosophy along the lines indicated by M. Le Roy, although we may expect — judging from his former books — that this will take the form, not of the formulation of a new moral code, but of the discovery of a new way of looking at life and appraising action.

HENRI BERGSON

Until recently the triumphal march of Bergson
into increasing popularity and influence has met
with little systematic opposition. Some have found
him obscure. Some have called him absurd. He
has his devoted partisans and bitter opponents.
But his views have not yet been subjected to the
thorough criticism which they must inevitably
receive sooner or later. A step in this direction is
the study of the pragmatic movement by René
Berthelot. The first volume of his "Utilitarian
Romanticism" deals, with the pragmatism of
Nietzsche and Poincaré; the second with the pragmatism of Bergson. The author, after the manner
of historians of philosophy, is more concerned to
determine what is new in Bergson than what is
true. He acts upon the old military rule "divide
and conquer" and accordingly splits up Bergson-
ism into German romanticism and Anglo-Saxon
utilitarianism, and then proceeds to dispatch these
severally after the orthodox manner. This proce-
dure is in a way begging the question, for it implicitly
denies the Bergsonian thesis that there may be something new in the world. Tracing a thing back to
its roots is all very well, provided that you do not
assume that the roots are all there is of the plant
that has grown out of them.

[89]

In tracing this genealogy of thought M. Berthelot finds Bergson related to Nietzsche on the romantic side. Both, he says, derive their romanticism from Schelling; Bergson, through his revered teacher, Ravaisson, and Nietzsche through Hoelderlin, Emerson, Schopenhauer, and Wagner. "Like the symbolists, Nietzsche and Bergson have drunk in different cups the water from the same magic fountain; an invisible Vivian has bound them both in the same enchantment."

From the other side of the house — might we say the masculine side? — Bergson derived his utilitarian empiricism; M. Berthelot traces its descent from Berkeley through Hume, Mill, Bain, and Spencer. In the course of this discussion the author introduces the following ingenious formula:

Hobbes : Berkeley : : Nietzsche : Bergson.

Those who are sufficiently expert with the application of the rule of three to metaphysics may work this out at their leisure.

One would suppose, on Mendelian principles, that a hybrid of such diverse and distinguished intellectual ancestry would show more originality than Berthelot is willing to allow to Bergson. At the end of his analysis he comes to the conclusion that

HENRI BERGSON

Bergson has really made only one important contribution to philosophy; that is, his conception of duration as distinguished from time. As Berkeley in analyzing the idea of space showed how psychological space, that is, the notion of space derived from sensation, differed from mathematical or formal space, so Bergson has shown how concrete duration or psychological time differs from mathematical or formal time. But even this theory according to our author is misapplied by Bergson, for it is not an opposition between space and time, but between two different conceptions of both space and time. This is characteristic of Berthelot's criticism, which is mainly directed toward breaking down all along the line the dichotomy to which Bergson is addicted.

Bergson's literary skill and amazing popularity seem to annoy him as they do other professors of philosophy in various lands. Whenever Berthelot presents Bergson with a bundle of compliments, we may detect a nettle hidden in the bouquet, as when he alludes to Bergson as "the Debussy of contemporary philosophy", and he says that with an increasing floridity of style the number of the *bergsoniennes* has come to surpass that of the *bergsoniens*. But that a philosophy should become fashionable seems to me rather creditable to the public than discreditable to the originator.

Professor Bergson has on several occasions expressed an interest in the efforts of the Society of Psychical Research to throw light into dark corners, and he has shown his sympathy by accepting the presidency of the English society, a successor in that position to F. W. H. Myers, Sir Oliver Lodge, Sir William Crookes, A. J. Balfour, and Andrew Lang. In his presidential address delivered in Æolian Hall, London, May 28, 1913, Professor Bergson made the novel suggestion that if the same amount of effort had been given toward the study of mental phenomena as has been given to physical, we might now know as much about mind as we do about matter. The concluding passage of the address is worth quoting:

What would have happened if all our science, for three centuries past, had been directed toward the knowledge of the mind, instead of toward that of matter — if, for instance, Kepler and Galileo and Newton had been psychologists ? Psychology would have attained developments of which one could no more form an idea than people had been able, before Kepler and Galileo and Newton, to form an idea of our astronomy and of our physics. Probably, instead of their being disdained *a priori*, all the strange facts with which psychical research was concerned would have been sought out minutely. Probably we should have had a vitalist biology quite different from ours, perhaps also a different medicine, or therapeutics by way of suggestion would have been pushed to a point of which we can form no idea. But when the human mind, having pushed thus far the science of mind, had turned toward inert matter, it would have been confused as to its direction, not knowing how to set to work, not knowing how to apply to this matter the processes with which it had been successful up till then. The world of physical, and not that of psychical, phenomena would then have been the world of mystery. It was, however, neither possible nor desirable that things should have happened thus. It was not possible, because at the dawn of modern times mathematical science already existed, and it was necessary, consequently, that the mind should pursue its researches in a direction to which that science was applicable. Nor was it desirable, even for the science of mind, for there would always have been wanting to that science something infinitely precious — the precision, the anxiety for proof, the habit of distinguishing that which is certain and that which is simply possible or probable. The sciences concerned with matter can alone give to the mind that precision, that rigor, those scruples. Let us now approach the science of mind with these excellent habits, renouncing the bad metaphysic which embarrasses our research, and the science of the mind will attain results surpassing all our hopes.

But whatever might have been the result if Kepler, Galileo, and Newton had turned their attention to psychology instead of physics, it must be confessed that the Society for Psychical Research has been a disappointment, notwithstanding that it has numbered among its zealous investigators such distinguished scientists as Lodge, Crookes, and Wallace. When the society was organized in 1882, its first president, Professor Sidgwick, called attention to the numerous reports of physical phenomena in the séance room and expressed the hope that such evidence would be forthcoming more abundantly now that competent investigators were prepared to deal with them. But quite the contrary happened. As Mr. Podmore puts it in his book on "The Naturalization of the Supernatural":

"In short, just when an organized and systematic investigation on a scale not inadequate to the importance of the subject was for the first time about to be made, the phenomena to be investigated diminished rapidly in frequency and importance, and the opportunities for investigation were further curtailed by the indifference or reluctance of the mediums to submit their claims to investigation."

It would seem, then, that since mankind, or some small portion of it, has acquired the precision, rigor, and scruples of physical science, it has become difficult, even impossible, to cultivate the occult. Still most of us would agree with M. Bergson that, assuming that there was such an alternative opened to humanity as he supposes, science has chosen the better part in undertaking the conquest of the physical world first.

The religious importance of Bergson's theory of evolution will be apparent from the quotations given. It has occurred to me in reading his later work that in some passages the word "faith" could be substituted for "philosophy", and "*elohim*" for "*élan vital*", without materially altering the sense. Then, too, his emphasis of time restores a conception which has always been a vital factor in religious faith, but which is not found in the scientific conception of the world as a reversible reaction or the metaphysical conception of the world as an illusion of an unchangeable Absolute. The present day is different from any other, and the future depends upon it. We cannot console or excuse ourselves by saying, "It will be all the same a hundred years hence." Now is the accepted time, the day of decision, the unique opportunity, and the election may be irrevocable, a turning point in the history of the creation. The atoms have lost their chance. The animals are hopelessly sidetracked. Upon us depends the future, the salvation of the world.

We must no longer speak of life in general as if it were an abstraction, or a mere rubric under which all living beings are enrolled. At a certain time, in certain points of space, a very visible current originated. This current of life, traversing the bodies which it has successively organized, passing from generation to generation, has divided itself among species and dispersed itself among individuals without losing anything of its force. — "Creative Evolution."

Bergson's philosophy would apparently lead to a conception of God more Arminian than Calvinistic, if it is permissible to apply the old theological categories; a God perhaps conscious, personal, and anthropomorphic, but not omnipotent and unchangeable. In fact it has a striking similarity to the conception of the Alexandrian Gnostics, a creative force struggling against the intractability of inert matter and triumphing by subtlety and persistence. The motto of Louis XI, *Divide et impera*, applies here in a different sense:

God, thus defined, has nothing of the already made: He is unceasing life, action, freedom. Creation, so conceived, is not a mystery; we experience it in ourselves when we act freely. . . .

It is as if a vague and formless being whom we may call as we will, man or superman, had sought to realize himself, and had succeeded only by abandoning part of himself on the way. The losses are represented by the rest of the animal world and even

by the vegetable world. — "Creative Evolution",
pp. 248, 266.

According to this view, the world is gradually
coming to life, acquiring a consciousness. Matter
is an Undine in search of a soul. A Rodin statue
with human forms emerging from the unhewn stone
is Bergson's philosophy in marble. We see again
Milton's " tawny lion pawing to get free his hinder
parts." We hear again Faust's translation of the
Logos : "In the beginning was the Act."

But I must refrain from imposing such analogies
upon an author who has taken pains to clothe his
thought in fresh language in order to be free from
the connotations of the old. Let Bergson summarize
his theory of evolution in his own words :

Life as a whole, from the initial impulsion that
thrust it into the world, will appear as a wave that
rises, and which is opposed by the descending movement of matter. On the greater part of its surface,
at different heights, the current is converted by matter
into a vortex. At one point alone it passes freely,
dragging with it the obstacle which will weigh on its
progress but will not stop it. At this point is humanity ; it is our privileged situation. On the other hand,
this rising wave is consciousness, and, like all consciousness, it includes potentialities without number
which interpenetrate and to which consequently
neither the category of unity nor that of multiplicity
is appropriate, made as they both are for inert matter.

The matter that it bears along with it, and in the interstices of which it inserts itself, alone can divide it into distinct individualities. On flows the current, running through human generations, subdividing itself into individuals. This subdivision was vaguely indicated in it, but could not have been made clear without matter. Thus souls are continually being created, which, nevertheless, in a certain sense pre-existed. They are nothing else than the little rills into which the great river of life divides itself, flowing through the body of humanity. The movement of the stream is distinct from the river bed, although it must adopt its winding course. Consciousness is distinct from the organism it animates, although it must undergo its vicissitudes. As the possible actions which a state of consciousness indicates are at every instant beginning to be carried out in the nervous centers, the brain underlines at every instant the motor indications of the state of consciousness; but the interdependency of consciousness and brain is limited to this; the destiny of consciousness is not bound up on that account with the destiny of cerebral matter. Finally, consciousness is essentially free; it is freedom itself; but it cannot pass through matter without settling on it, without adapting itself to it; this adaptation is what we call intellectuality; and the intellect, turning itself back toward active, that is to say, free, consciousness, naturally makes it enter into the conceptual forms into which it is accustomed to see matter fit. It will, therefore, always perceive freedom in the form of necessity; it will always neglect the part of novelty or of creation inherent in free act; it will always substitute for action itself an imitation, artificial, approximate, obtained by compounding the old with the old and the same with the same. Thus, to the eyes of a philosophy that attempts to reabsorb intellect in intuition, many difficulties vanish or become light. But such a doctrine does not only facilitate speculation, it gives us also more power to act and to live. For, with it, we feel ourselves no longer isolated in humanity, humanity no longer seems isolated in the nature that it dominates. As the smallest grain of dust is bound up with our entire solar system, drawn along with it in that undivided movement of descent which is materiality itself, so all organized beings, from the humblest to the highest, from the first origins of life to the time in which we are, and in all places as in all times, do but evidence a single impulsion, the inverse of the movement of matter, and in itself indivisible. All the living hold together, and all yield to the same tremendous push. The animal takes its stand on the plant, man bestrides animality, and the whole of humanity, in space and in time, is one immense army galloping beside and before and behind each of us in an overwhelming charge able to beat down every resistance and clear the most formidable obstacles, perhaps even death. — "Creative Evolution", p. 269.

How to Read Bergson

Read the last first. Begin with "Creative Evolution", for this is the most comprehensive exposition of his philosophy and is written in a less technical style than his earlier works. But the reader must remember that a knowledge of these is presupposed, and Bergson has here taken for granted what he has written two other large volumes to prove; namely, that time cannot be adequately represented in the forms of space, and that mind is not rigidly bound to matter. Bergson is unexcelled by any modern philosopher except William James in brilliancy of style and originality of illustration. "Creative Evolution" treats of such a variety of questions, biological, psychological, and metaphysical, that any intelligent reader will find something in it that will arouse new trains of thought. And if the intelligent reader finds passages which he cannot understand, he may console himself with the reflection that there are others who have been likewise baffled. Count Keyserling, who has the brain of a German metaphysician, says of Bergson that "his philosophy is perhaps the most original achievement since the days of Immanuel Kant", but he adds, "Many thoughts on which Bergson appears to lay great weight arouse in me not the shade of an idea." But he ascribes Bergson's obscurity to the fact that "he does not start from abstract principles; he begins in direct consciousness, in concrete life", so perhaps the ordinary reader may have in this respect an advantage over a Kantian student like Count Keyserling.

The student of philosophy may prefer to trace the development of Bergson's thought in its logical and chronological order. He will in that case begin with the " Essài sur les données immédiates de la conscience" (1889), and proceed to "Matière et Mémoire" (1896), and end with " Evolution créatrice " (1907). These are published by Félix Alcan, Paris, in his " Bibliothèque de Philosophie contemporaine." The "Essay on the Immediate Data of Consciousness" appears under the less cumbrous title of "Time and Free Will" in the translation of F. L. Pogson (Mac-

millan). "Matter and Memory" is translated by
Nancy Margaret Paul and W. Scott Palmer (Mac-
millan). It may not be improper to note that the
British edition of the Essay costs nearly four times
as much as the French and is twice as heavy. "Crea-
tive Evolution", translated by Arthur Mitchell, is
printed in this country by Henry Holt & Company.
Bergson's lecture on Dreams, translated by E. E.
Slosson, is published in book form by B. W. Huebsch,
New York.

Those who read French but do not wish to attack
one of the larger works will find convenient the
summary of his philosophy with illustrative selec-
tions made by one of his former pupils, René Gillouin,
and published in "Les Grands Philosophes" by Louis
Michaud, Paris. The German reader will find in
A. Steenbergen's "Bergsons Intuitive Philosophie",
Jena, an epitome and critique.

"Time and Free Will" contains an admirable
bibliography, including the most important discussions of Bergson's philosophy that have appeared
in eight languages up to 1911. The most interesting
introduction to Bergson is the article published by
Professor James in the *Hibbert Journal*, April, 1909,
and reprinted in his *Pluralistic Universe*. This has
the advantage of M. Bergson's indorsement, for
when Professor Pitkin of Columbia attempted to
show that James was wrong in claiming Bergson as
an ally ("James and Bergson, or Who is Against
Intellect ?" in *Journal of Philosophy, Psychology and
Scientific Method*, April 28, 1910), Bergson replied
that James had not misinterpreted him but had said
what he meant in better words than his (same *Journal*, July 7, 1910). Other brief expositions of Bergson's philosophy are the articles by H. Wildon Carr

in *Proc. Aristotelian Society*, 1909 and 1910, and *Hibbert Journal*, July, 1910; by J. Solomon in *Mind*, January, 1911 (both these now in book form also); by Arthur Balfour on "Creative Evolution and Philosophic Doubt" in the decennial number of the *Hibbert Journal;* "Bergson's Philosophy and the Idea of God," by H. C. Corrance, and "Syndicalism in its Relation to Bergson," by T. Rhondda Williams, both in *Hibbert Journal* of January, 1914. Professor Arthur O. Lovejoy of Johns Hopkins criticizes "The Practical Tendencies of Bergsonianism" in the *International Journal of Ethics*, April and July, 1913. Bergson's London lectures on the soul are summarized in the *Educational Review*, January, 1912. Santayana's "Winds of Doctrine" (Scribner) contains an interesting chapter on Bergson's philosophy.

Of the voluminous controversial literature in France it is only possible to mention a few recent titles : R. Gillouin, "La Philosophie de Bergson" (Grasset) ; J. Segond, "L'Intuition Bergsonienne" (Alcan) ; J. Desaymard, "La Pensée d'Henri Bergson" (Mercure de France). The most conspicuous of the opponents of Bergson are : René Berthelot in "Un Romanticisme utilitaire," tome II, "Le Pragmatisme chez Bergson" (Alcan) ; and Julien Benda in "Le Bergsonisme ou une Philosophie de la Mobilité", and "Réponse aux Defenseurs du Bergsonisme" (Mercure de France).

"Bergson for Beginners", by Darcy B. Kitchin (Macmillan) gives a summary of his works and adds some interesting observations on the relation of Bergson to 'the English philosophers James Ward and Herbert Spencer. Other recent expositions and criticisms are "The Philosophy of Bergson", by A. D. Lindsay; "A Critical Examination of Bergson's

Philosophy ", by J. McKellar Stewart; "An Exam-
ination of Professor Bergson's Philosophy ", by
David Balsillie; "Bergson and the Modern Spirit ",
by G. R. Dodgson (American Unitarian Assoc.,
Boston). But the best volume to serve as an intro-
duction to Bergson is that previously mentioned,
"The New Philosophy of Henri Bergson ", by
Edouard Le Roy (Holt).

A list of the most important of the books and
articles on the subject in all languages up to 1913
comprising more than five hundred titles was published by the Columbia University Press on the occasion of Bergson's visit, "A Contribution to a Bibliography of Henri Bergson."

CHAPTER III

HENRI POINCARÉ

The scientist does not study nature because it is useful; he studies it because he delights in it, and he delights in it because it is beautiful. If nature were not beautiful, it would not be worth knowing, and if nature were not worth knowing, life would not be worth living. Of course I do not here speak of that beauty that strikes the senses, the beauty of qualities and of appearances; not that I undervalue such beauty, far from it, but it has nothing to do with science; I mean that profounder beauty which comes from the harmonious order of the parts, and which a pure intelligence can grasp. This it is which gives body, a structure so to speak, to the iridescent appearances which flatter our senses, and without this support the beauty of these fugitive dreams would be only imperfect, because it would be vague and always fleeting. On the contrary, intellectual beauty is sufficient unto itself, and it is for its sake, more perhaps than for the future good of humanity, that the scientist devotes himself to long and difficult labors.

It is, therefore, the quest of this special beauty, the sense of the harmony of the cosmos, which makes us choose the facts most fitting to contribute to this harmony, just as an artist chooses from among the features of his model those which perfect the picture and give it character and life. And we need not fear that this instinctive and unavowed prepossession will turn the scientist aside from the search for the true. One may dream a harmonious world, but how far the real world will leave it behind! The greatest artists that ever lived, the Greeks, made their heavens; how shabby it is beside the true heavens, ours! — Poincaré's "The Value of Science," p. 8.

SUCH language as this is extremely disconcerting to those who hold the popular notion of science and scientists; regarding science as a vague impending mass of solid fact, immutable, inexorable, threatening the extinction of all such things as art, sentiment, poetry, and religion, only to be diverted by a determination to remain ignorant of it; regarding men of science as mere calculating machines, mechanically grinding out logical grist for utilitarian purposes. Mathematical astronomy is surely one of the sciences, the most rigid, remote, and recondite of the sciences. Yet here is the leading mathematical astronomer of the age talking about it as though it were one of the fine arts, a thing of beauty that the artist creates for his own delight in the making of it and shapes in accordance with his own ideas of what is harmonious.

Now we cannot throw out of consideration M. Poincaré's opinion, on the ground that he did not know what he was talking about. A man who has made as much science as he has ought to know how science is made, and what for. To most of us nature — or to avoid hurting our own feelings let us rather say, opportunity — has denied the privilege of knowing this by experience. Consequently M. Poincaré is an especially interesting man to study, for he has been willing to tell us not only what a man of science is, but also how it feels to be one. No other contemporary of equal eminence has been so frank and accommodating in the self-revelation of his methods or so willing to submit himself as a subject of observation. We are admitted to the laboratory of a mathematician, and we can watch the mechanism of scientific thought in action.

So far as he is concerned, he has repudiated the idea that science is purely utilitarian in the most emphatic language. August Comte said that it would be idle to seek to know the composition of the sun, since this knowledge would be of no use to sociology. Against such a charge of uselessness Poincaré eloquently defended his science by showing the practical value of astronomy even from Comte's point of view, but in conclusion asserted his own opinion very plainly:

Was I wrong in saying that it is astronomy which has made us a soul capable of comprehending nature;

that under heavens always overcast and starless, the earth itself would have been for us eternally unintelligible; that we should there have seen only caprice and disorder; and that, not knowing the world, we should never have been able to subdue it? What science could have been more useful? And in thus speaking I put myself at the point of view of those who only value practical applications. Certainly, this point of view is not mine; as for me, on the contrary, if I admire the conquests of industry, it is, above all, because they free us from material cares, they will one day give to all the leisure to contemplate nature. I do not say: Science is useful, because it teaches us to construct machines. I say: Machines are useful, because in working for us, they will some day leave us more time to make science. But finally it is worth remarking that between the two points of view there is no antagonism, and that man having pursued a disinterested aim, all else has been added unto him. — "Value of Science", p. 88.

It is this insistence upon the æsthetic value of science that caused him to shrink from being called a "pragmatist", although those who accept that name have always laid unusual stress upon the æsthetic factor in thinking. But in his theory of knowledge Poincaré is decidedly pragmatic, and no one has given a clear exposition or stronger expression to the practical mode of thought by which the natural sciences have made their progress and which is now being extended to the fields of metaphysics, religion, ethics, and sociology. Poincaré's favorite word is "convenient" (*commode*). Theories are strictly speaking not to be classed as true or false. They are merely more or less convenient. For example:

Masses are coefficients it is convenient to introduce into calculations. We could reconstruct all mechanics by attributing different values to all the masses. This new mechanics would not be in contradiction either with experience or with the general principles of dynamics. Only the equations of this new mechanics would be *less simple.* — "Science and Hypothesis", p. 76.

We have not a direct intuition of simultaneity, nor of the equality of two durations. If we think we have this intuition, this is an illusion. We replace it by the aid of certain rules which we apply almost always without taking count of them. But what is the nature of these rules? No general rule, no rigorous rule; a multitude of little rules applicable to each particular case. These rules are not imposed upon us, and we might amuse ourselves by inventing others; but they could not be cast aside without greatly complicating the laws of physics, mathematics, and astronomy. We therefore choose these rules, not because they are true, but because they are most convenient, and we may recapitulate them as follows: "The simultaneity of two events or the order of their succession, the equality of two durations, are to be so defined that the enunciation of the natural laws may be as simple as possible; in other words, all these rules, all these definitions, are only the fruit of an unconscious opportunism." — "Value of Science", p. 35.

HENRI POINCARÉ

Time should be so defined that the equations of mechanics may be as simple as possible. In other words, there is not one way of measuring time more true than another. That which is generally adopted is only more *convenient.* Of two watches, we have no right to say that one goes true, the other wrong: we can only say that it is advantageous to conform to the indications of the first. — "Value of Science", p. 30.

Behold then the rule we follow and the only one we can follow: when a phenomenon appears to us as the cause of another, we regard it as anterior. It is therefore by cause we define time. — "Value of Science", p. 32.

Experience does not prove to us that space has three dimensions. It only proves to us that it is convenient to attribute three dimensions to it. — "Value of Science", p. 69.

It has often been observed that if all the bodies in the universe were dilated simultaneously and in the same proportion we should have no means of perceiving it, since all our measuring instruments would grow at the same time as the objects themselves which they serve to measure. The world, after this dilatation, would continue on its course without anything apprising us of so considerable an event. — "Value of Science", p. 39.

But Poincaré goes farther and shows not only that two such worlds of different sizes would be absolutely indistinguishable, but that they would be equally indistinguishable if they were distorted in any manner so long as they corresponded with each other point by point. This conception of the relativity of space may be thought a little hard to grasp, but M. Poincaré is kind enough to suggest a way by which any one may see it for himself if he has ten cents to admit him to one of those hilarious resorts where life-size concave and convex mirrors are to be seen.[1] You may think yourself a gentleman of proper figure, that is to say, somewhat portly, and you look upon the tall slim shape that confronts you in the cylindrical mirror as absurdly misshapen. But you would find it difficult to convince him of his deformity. His legs, as well as yours, fulfill the requirement that Lincoln laid down as their proper length; that is, they reach from the body to the ground. If you touch your chin with your thumb and your brow with your forefinger, so does he. It occurs to you that here is a case where your knowledge of geometry would, if ever, prove useful, but when you appeal to it, you will find that the geometry of his queer-looking world is just as good as yours; in fact, is just the same. You get a foot rule and measure yourself; 70 inches high, 14 inches in diameter at the equator, ratio 5 : 2. But meanwhile the mirror man is also measuring himself, and his dimensions come out exactly the same as yours, 70 and 14 and 5 : 2, for when he

[1] "Science et Méthode," p. 101.

holds the rule perpendicular it lengthens and when horizontal it shrinks. Lines that in your world are straight are curved in his, but you cannot prove it to him, for when he lays his straightedge against these curves of his, behold it immediately bends to correspond. By this time, finding it so difficult to prove to the mirror man that you are right and he is wrong, it occurs to you that perhaps he isn't, that he may have just as much reason as you for believing that his is the normal, well-proportioned world, and yours the distorted image of it. Since, then, you have no way of perceiving the absolute length, direction, or curvature of a line, your space may be as irregularly curved and twisted as it looks to be in the funniest of the mirrors, and you would not know it. Now the principle of the pragmatist is that anything that does not make any difference to anything else is not real. The reason why we have not been able to discover any differences between the mirror space and our space, each considered by itself, is because there is none. Or to return to the language of Poincaré, "space is in reality amorphous and the things that are in it alone give it a form." Why do we say that space has three dimensions instead of two or four or more? Why do we stick to an old fogy like Euclid when Riemann and Lobachevski proffer us new and equally self-consistent systems of geometry wherein parallels may meet or part ?   Because :

by natural selection our mind has *adapted* itself to the conditions of the external world.   It has adopted the geometry *most advantageous* to the species or, in other words, *the most convenient.*   Geometry is not true, it is advantageous.

Such language may pass without notice in university halls, for all scientists are more or less clearly conscious of the provisional and practical nature of the hypotheses and conventions they employ. But to the outside world it sounds startling.   To some it seemed that the foundations of the universe were being undermined.   Others saw in it a confession of what Brunetière had called "the bankruptcy of science" and openly rejoiced over the discomfiture of the enemy of the Church.   Now Poincaré had chanced to use in discussing the relativity of motion the following illustration :

Absolute space, that is to say, the mark to which it would be necessary to refer the earth to know whether it really moves, has no objective existence. Hence this affirmation "the earth turns round" has no meaning, since it can be verified by no experiment; since such an experiment not only could not be either realized or dreamed by the boldest Jules

Verne but cannot be conceived of without contradiction. Or rather these two propositions: "The
earth turns round" and "it is more convenient to suppose the earth turns round" have the same meaning;
there is nothing more in the one than in the other.
— "Science and Hypothesis", p. 85.

This remark was at once seized upon by the Catholic apologists, and the Galileo case, once closed by
the voice of Rome, was reopened for the admission
of this new evidence. If the Ptolemaic and the
Copernican theories are equally true, and the choice
between them is merely a matter of expediency,
was not the Holy Inquisition justified in upholding
the established theory in the interests of religion and
morality? Monsignor Bolo, an eminent and saga-
cious theologian, announced in *Le Matin* of February 20, 1908, that M. Poincaré, the greatest mathematician of the century, says that Galileo was
wrong in his obstinacy. To this Poincaré replied
in the whispered words of Galileo:

"E pur si muove, Monseigneur."

In a later discussion of the point, he explains that
what he said about the rotation of the earth could
be equally well applied to any other accepted hypothesis, even the very existence of an external world,
for "these two propositions, 'the external world
exists' or 'it is more convenient to suppose that it

exists' have one and the same meaning." The Copernican theory is the preferable because it has a richer, more profound content, since if we assume the earth is stationary we have to invent other explanations for the flattening at the poles, the rotation of Foucault's pendulum, the trade winds, etc., while the hypothesis of a revolving earth brings all these together as the effects of a single cause.

M. Le Roy, a Catholic pragmatist and a disciple of Bergson's, goes much further than Poincaré in regard to the human element in science, holding that science is merely a rule of action and can teach us nothing of truth, for its laws are only artificial conventions. This view Poincaré considered to be dangerously near to absolute nominalism and skepticism, and in his controversy with Le Roy [1] he showed that the scientist does not "create facts as Le Roy said, but merely the language in which he enunciates them." Of the contingence upon which Le Roy and Boutroux insist, Poincaré would admit only that scientific laws can never be more than approximate and probable. Even in astronomy, where the single and simple law of gravitation is involved, neither absolute certainty nor absolute accuracy can be attained. Therefore we cannot

[1] Part III of "The Value of Science."

Votre bien dévoué

Poincaré

safely say that at a particular time Saturn will be at a certain point in the heavens. We must limit ourselves to the prediction that "Saturn will *probably* be *near*" such a point.

In an address before the International Philosophical Congress at Bologna in April, 1910, Professor Poincaré discussed again the question of whether the laws of nature may not change. He admitted that there is not a sole law that we can enunciate with the certainty that it has always been true in the past. Nevertheless, he concluded, there is nothing to hinder the man of science from keeping his faith in the principle of immutability, since no law can descend to the level of a secondary and limited law without being replaced by another law more general and more comprehensive. He considered in particular the possibility that in the remote past the fundamental laws of mechanics would not hold, for since the energy of the world has been continually dissipating in the form of heat there must have been a time when bodies moved faster than they do now. But according to the recent theories of matter, no body can travel faster than light, and with velocities approaching that of light its mass is no longer constant but increases with its velocity. This, of course, would play havoc with all of Newton's laws, which then we should have to regard as limited in their scope to such ordinary conditions and moderate motion as we see about us now.

But even at present we can hardly regard them with the same implicit confidence as formerly. Take, for example, Newton's law that action and reaction are equal and opposite. When a ball is fired from a cannon, the cannon recoils at the same time and with the same momentum that the ball goes forward. But suppose instead of a cannon we have a lamp with a reflector sending a beam of light into space. It has been deduced mathematically and proved experimentally that light exerts a minute but measurable pressure on an object which it strikes. The reflector therefore recoils like the cannon, but where is the ball if light is an immaterial wave motion? To be sure, if the ray of light strikes some planet out in space, it would give it an impulse equal and opposite to that originally imparted to the reflector on our earth. But what if the light goes on through vacant space and never hits anything at all? A law that may have to wait several thousand years for its validation and may even fail of it altogether is not what the layman has in mind when he thinks of immutable and infrangible laws governing the universe.

But it is rather important just now that the lay-man gets to understand what the scientist means when he talks of laws, theories, and hypotheses. For we are in the midst of a stupendous revolution in science. Our nicely arranged nineteenth century cosmos seems to be dissolving into chaos again. We have seen the elements melt with fervent heat and we can no longer rely upon the uniformity of atomic weights. The laws of the conservation of matter and energy, which were the guiding stars of research to the last generation, are becoming dimmed. The old-fashioned ether, in its time a useful but never entirely satisfactory contrivance, for it had to be patched up repeatedly with divers new properties to enable it to bear the various duties thrust upon it, seems no longer competent to stand the strain and may have to be sent to the scientific scrap-heap at any moment. We hear physicists of supposed sanity assert that all bodies contract in the direction of their motion and that their weight varies with their speed and the direction in which they are going. We read of "atoms of light," and of corpuscles of electricity which, though they are but a thousandth part of the hydrogen atom, are caught and counted and weighed one by one.

Now what puzzles the lay mind is the calmness

with which the scientists survey this crash of worlds
and shock of systems. They do not have the mien
of exposed impostors. They are not, like the augurs
of decadent Rome, unable to meet without laughing
in each other's faces. They do not resent the overthrow of their former idols. They have no fear
of heretics, consequently no hatred for them. They
regard all this iconoclasm with a mild curiosity
quite in contrast to their intense and personal interest in science generally. It is hard to get out
a quorum at the Association for the Advancement
of Science to hear a discussion of the principle of
relativity with all its revolutionary consequences.

Compare this apparent indifference to the fate
of fundamental principles in scientific circles with
what would happen in a Presbyterian assembly if
it should be proposed to eliminate predestination
from the Westminster Confession or in an Episcopal
convocation if the Virgin Birth were denied; with
what would happen in a stockholders' meeting if
doubt were expressed as to the rights of capital, or
in a socialist convention if the class conflict were
questioned. Now the existence of the ether has
the same importance to scientific thought that predestination has to theological or capitalism to economic thought. Its refutation or modification would

be quite as upsetting to faith and practice. Yet scientists are men; they have red blood in their veins, and it not infrequently shows in their cheeks when they debate something that seems to them worth while. Pure theory rarely seems to them worth while because it is recognized as pure conventionality and convenience.

The scientific man, especially the scientific investigator, holds his theories with a light hand, but keeps a firm grip on his facts. This is just the opposite of the lay attitude toward science. If the layman is interested in knowing the speed of light, it is because he thinks that he learns from it that all space is filled with a rigid elastic solid, at which he cannot but wonder. The scientist is interested in the ether because it helps him in his calculation of the speed of light.

A lecturer on wireless telegraphy will use in the course of the hour two or three more or less contradictory conceptions of electricity. If afterward you call his attention to the inconsistency and ask him which is right and which is wrong, you will not get a very satisfactory answer. He does not know and obviously does not care. You insist upon his telling you which theory he personally believes in. He really had not thought of "believing" in any of them. If he uses white chalk on the blackboard in preference to red, it is not because he denies the existence of red chalk and its occasional usefulness. So, too, the astronomer will speak of the sun's rising and in the next breath of the earth's turning toward the sun, quite innocent of his inconsistency. The botanist alludes to a certain flower as a poppy and again as Eschscholtzia. He means the same thing but is using different languages; in the first case English, in the second case I don't know what.

It is eminently desirable that people should have faith in science, but in order to do that they must have the same sort of faith in it that the scientist has. Otherwise they will regard it as a lot of ingenious fancies which are proved false by each succeeding generation. Science is moulting just now and looks queer. The public ought to understand clearly that the process means growth and not disease. There is another reason now for the popularization of the scientific mode of thought. It is beginning to be applied where entirely different conceptions have so far prevailed — to art, ethics, religion, sociology, and the like. This is already arousing a great commotion and will cause more before the process is complete. It will, for example, involve the rewriting and to a large extent the reinvestigation of history. Poincaré has hinted at this in a passage which seems to me of very great significance:

> Carlyle has somewhere said something like this: "Nothing but facts are of importance. John Lackland passed by here. Here is something that is admirable. Here is a reality for which I would give all the theories in the world." Carlyle was a fellow countryman of Bacon, but Bacon would not have said that. That is the language of the historian. The physicist would say rather: "John Lackland passed by here. That makes no difference to me for he never will pass this way again." — "Science and Hypothesis", p. 102.

The aim of science is prevision, and I believe that this will eventually be recognized as the true aim of all knowledge. The historian, or let me say rather the antiquarian, for the historian may have the scientific temperament, values facts for their rarity. The scientist values facts for their commonness. A unique fact, if there be such, would have no possible interest to him. The antiquarian goes about looking for things, facts, or furniture, which have been of importance in the past. The scientist is looking only for things that will be of importance in the future.

According to Poincaré, the proper choice of facts

is the first duty of the scientist. He must be able to pick out the significant and reject all the rest. "Invention consists in avoiding the constructing of useless combinations and in constructing the useful combinations which are in infinite minority. To invent is to discern, to choose." It is most desirable to bring together elements far distant from one another. Such unions are mostly sterile, but when this is not the case, they are the most fruitful of all. The successful scientist does not, like a shopper, look over one by one all available samples and pick out what he wants. Life is too short. The unsuitable ideas do not even present themselves to his mind. It is as if he were an examiner of second resort who only concerns himself with the candidates who have passed the first test. This preliminary sifting and sorting process is done largely by the unconscious mind, as Poincaré shows by telling how he came to make his first mathematical discoveries:

For a fortnight I labored to demonstrate that there could exist no function analogous to those that I have since called the fuchsian functions.[1] I was then

[1] M. Poincaré, in relating these experiences for their psychological interest, was kind enough to say that the non-mathematical reader need not be frightened at these barbarous names, for it is not at all necessary for him to know what they mean.

very ignorant. Every day I seated myself at my work table and spent an hour or two there, trying a great many combinations, but I arrived at no result. One night when, contrary to my custom, I had taken black coffee and I could not sleep, ideas surged up in crowds. I felt them as they struck against one another until two of them stuck together, so to speak, to form a stable combination. By morning I had established the existence of a class of fuchsian functions, those which are derived from the hypergeometric series. I had merely to put the results in shape, which only took a few hours. — "Science et Méthode", p. 52.

After working out the deductions from this discovery, he went on a geological excursion of the School of Mines. The distractions of travel took his mind from his mathematical labor. But at Constance, just as he was stepping into an omnibus for some excursion, the idea occurred to him, without any connection with his previous thoughts, that his fuchsian functions were identical in their transformations with those of the non-Euclidian geometry. He took his seat in the omnibus and continued his conversation, feeling absolutely certain of his discovery, which he worked out at his leisure on his return to his home at Caen.

He next devoted himself to the study of arithmetical questions, without reaching any results of importance and without suspecting that this subject could have the slightest connection with his earlier researches. Disgusted at his lack of success, he went to pass some days at the seashore, where he was occupied with other things. One day as he was walking on the cliff, the thought came to him, brief, sudden, and certain as usual, that he had been employing the same transformations in his arithmetical and geometrical work.

He thereupon went back to Caen and undertook the systematic application of his theory. But he was stopped by an insurmountable obstacle, and while in this perplexity he was called away to his military service at Mont-Valérien, where he had no time for mathematics. One day while walking on the street, the solution of the difficulty appeared to him in a flash. He did not try to think it out at the time, but after his release from the army, he completed his memoir without trouble.

These fascinating glimpses into the soul of a mathematician will remind the reader of many other instances of such subconscious assistance on record and doubtless of personal experiences as well. We think of Alfred Russel Wallace at Ternate, his brain inflamed with tropical fever, seized with the sudden inspiration of the theory of natural selection, the key to the biological problems which had perplexed him for so many months. How fortunate that his clerical opponents did not know of this and so could not dismiss evolution as the dream of a diseased imagination. But as James says in his "Varieties of Religious Experience", we have no right to discountenance unwelcome theories as feverish fancies, since for all we know 102° may be a more favorable temperature for truth to germinate and sprout in than the ordinary bloodheat of 98°.

We are reminded, too, of Kekulé of Bonn puzzling over the constitution of benzene, trying in vain to satisfy six carbon atoms with six hydrogen atoms when they wanted fourteen. In the evening as he sat by the fire, his wearied brain refused to rest, and he seemed to see the four-handed carbon imps dancing with their one-armed hydrogen partners on the floor. Suddenly six of them joined hands in a ring and the problem was solved. Since then the benzene sextet has been dancing through hundreds of volumes and has added millions annually to the wealth of Germany. Professor Hilprecht of the University of Pennsylvania has told how a Chaldean priest, custodian of the "Temple Library", appeared to him in a dream and showed him how to put together the fragments of a cuneiform inscription which he had for a long time been striving in vain to translate.

Then there was Stevenson in Samoa, writing for dear life, but not failing to give credit to his "brownies" for doing a large part of his work for him. But the brownies do not work unbidden, and they will not make bricks without straw. Poincaré insists upon the necessity of the preliminary period of conscious effort without which these subliminal inspirations never come and the subsequent period of verification, development, and application, without which they are fruitless. Such ideas came to him most often in the evening or morning when he was in bed and half awake. He did not regard the operations of his unconscious mind as merely mechanical. On the contrary, it is distinguished by the power of choice, selecting and presenting to the conscious ego only those combinations that seem profitable and important. This choice is made, in Poincaré's opinion, under the guidance of the artistic instinct.

The usual combinations are precisely the most beautiful; I mean those which can best charm that special sensibility which all mathematicians recognize but at which the profane are tempted to smile. Among the numerous combinations which the subliminal self has blindly formed, almost all are without interest and without utility. For that reason they have no action upon the æsthetic sensibility and never come into consciousness. Only those that are harmonious and consequently both useful and beautiful are capable of moving that special sensibility of the geometrician of which I spoke, and which, once excited, calls our attention to them and so gives them the chance to become conscious. — "Science et Méthode", p. 58.

Poincaré, if we may believe what he says on this point, was a poor chess player and absolutely incapable of adding up a column of figures correctly. But the reader should beware of the common fallacy of reversing a proposition of this kind and assuming that if he, too, makes mistakes in addition he has the mind of a great mathematician. Poincaré's memory was, however, exceptionally good, especially for figures and formulas. On returning from a walk he was able to recall the numbers of the carriages he had met. When he was in the Polytechnic School he followed the courses in mathematics without taking a note and without looking at the syllabus provided by the professor. He was a rapid mental calculator, using auditive imagery rather than visual. He associated colors with the sound of words.[1]

[1] Dr. Toulouse has devoted a volume of his series of medico-psychological studies of men of genius to observations on the memory, reaction time, mode of thinking, habits, and physiological constitution of Henri Poincaré (Paris: Flammarion).

In this connection may be quoted an anecdote told by M. Jules Sageret:[1] At a *conférence* in the Superior School of Telegraphy the director called upon him to discuss a very difficult problem in the propagation of the electric current. Poincaré complied and solved the problem without taking any time in preparation. After the *conférence* the director felicitated him on the solution. "Yes," said Poincaré, "I found the value of x, but is it in kilograms or kilometers?"

Poincaré did not find it profitable to work more than two hours at a time. His custom was to stay at his desk from ten o'clock to noon and from five to seven in the afternoon, never working in the evening after dinner. He drank wine at meals, but never smoked. He went to bed at ten and rose at seven, but did not sleep soundly.

He was a blond, five feet five inches in height and weighed 154 pounds. His head was unusually large, especially in breadth. His eyes were myopic and unsteady. He stood stoopingly with his wrinkled forehead upturned. He spoke somewhat slowly and with a distraught air, as though he were thinking of something else, even though he might be at the time interested and keenly observant.

[1] *Revue des Idées*, 1909, p. 488.

HENRI POINCARÉ

He talked English and German readily and read Latin and Italian. He was fond of music, especially Wagner.

Of the absent-mindedness that had been characteristic of him from youth, many stories are told. Like most mathematicians he was fond of walking while thinking, his fingers opening and closing in an unconscious gesture. One day on his return from a walk he was surprised to find that he was carrying a wicker cage, new and happily empty. He could not imagine how he had got it, but retracing his steps he found upon the sidewalk the stock of the basket maker whom he had innocently despoiled.

When as an engineering student he made a trip to Austria, his mother was afraid he would drop his portfolio sometime without noticing it. So, realizing doubtless that his memory was auditory, she sewed little bells on it. The plan was successful. His mother found on his return that he had brought back in his valise not only the portfolio but also an Austrian bed sheet neatly folded, which, some morning, he had mistaken for his night clothes.

These and similar anecdotes were told by M. Frédéric Masson when he welcomed M. Poincaré into the Académie Française, January 28, 1909,[1] and it must have been a trifle embarrassing to the new member to listen to such a minute analysis of his life and character addressed to him in the second person. How deftly the director of the Academy mingled eulogy and raillery may be seen from a quotation:

"You did not delay revealing your vocation and will be justly cited as the most precocious of infant prodigies. You were nine months old when for the first time as night came your eyes were directed toward the sky. You saw there a star light up. You persistently pointed it out to your mother, who was also your nurse. Then you discovered another with some astonishment, and your reason cried '*Enco lo la bas !*' A third, a fourth, more cries of joy and equal enthusiasm. You had to be put to bed because you became so excited discovering stars. That evening was your first contact with the infinite, and you had inaugurated your courses in astronomy, the youngest professor known."

Henri Poincaré was born April 29, 1854, at Nancy,

---

[1] Masson's address may be found in Le Bon's bibliography; also in *Popular Science Monthly*. An entertaining account of Poincaré's reception into the Academy was written for *Le Figaro* by André Beaunier and translated for the Boston *Transcript*.

where his ancestors had long been established. His grandfather was a pharmacist and his father a physician of more than usual scholarship. The name, he said, was originally Pontcaré, for, one can imagine a square bridge but not a square point. But the philologists who took the question up discovered in the register of the university a student named "Petrus Pugniquadrati" in 1403 and "Jehan Poingquarré" in 1418, so the name Poincaré meant "clenched-fist." His cousin, Raymond Poincaré, son of a distinguished engineer, has long been one of the most prominent figures in the political world, a member of the Academy, senator, minister, and is now president of the French republic.

In the Nancy *lycée* he led all his classes and showed a special aptitude for history and literature. At the age of thirteen he composed a five-act tragedy in verse, and since he was a Lorrainer, the heroine was of course Jeanne d'Arc. But as soon as he caught sight of a geometry, his true vocation became apparent. His instructor ran to his home and announced to his mother: "Madame, your son will be a mathematician."

Passing through the Polytechnic School he entered the National School of Mines, and for a few years after graduation he served as engineer in the

Government departments of mines and railroads. At the age of twenty-seven he was called to a chair of mathematics in the University of Paris, where he remained, also filling the positions of Professor of Astronomy in the Polytechnic School and Professor of Theoretical Electricity in the Professional School of Posts and Telegraphs. He was received into the Academy of Sciences at the early age of thirty-two, and at the time of his election to the French Academy he had been honored by election to membership by thirty-five foreign academies. He took his seat in the Académie française very appropriately as the successor of Sully-Prudhomme, who likewise was an engineer by profession and a philosopher by temperament. To Poincaré as well as to Sully-Prudhomme, science appealed to the æsthetic sense as a thing of beauty and an inspiration to the imagination.

He married at the age of twenty-seven and had four children, three daughters and a son. His younger sister is the wife of the philosopher, Émile Boutroux, well known in this country from the lectures he gave at Harvard and Princeton.

Poincaré was influential in introducing improved methods in teaching mathematics, promoting the use of natural and dynamical methods instead of the abstract and static methods of Euclid and Legendre. He was skeptical in regard to religion and indifferent to politics. When called upon to contribute to a symposium on the old question of the scholar in politics,[1] he responded that savants like all citizens ought to interest themselves in the affairs of the country. But politics has become a profession, and a savant who entered into it would have to devote half his time to public business if he would be useful and the other half to his constituents if he wished to keep his seat, so he would have no time for science.

When asked for his opinion on woman suffrage,[2] he replied as follows:

I see no theoretical reason for refusing the political suffrage to women, married or not. They pay taxes the same as men, and they contribute their sons, so it is even heavier upon them than upon men. Perhaps woman suffrage is the sole means of combating alcoholism. I fear only the clerical influence over women.

Of the achievements that have given M. Poincaré his world-wide fame I am not competent to speak. Readers who would know the significance and value of his work on fuchsian, hyper-fuchsian, theta-fuchsian, abelian, and elliptical functions must

[1] *Revue bleue*, June 4, 1907, p. 708.   [2] *La Revue*, 1910.

go further for the information. I can only quote the opinions of those most competent to express an opinion as to his contributions to science. In 1905 he received the Bolyai Prize of ten thousand crowns, which is awarded by the Hungarian Academy of Sciences every five years for the best work in mathematics done during that period. The official report by Gustave Rados begins as follows:

"Henri Poincaré is incontestably the first and most powerful investigator of the present time in the domain of mathematics and mathematical physics. His strongly marked individuality permits us to recognize in him a savant endowed with intuition, who knows how to draw from the exhaustless well of geometrical and mechanical intuitions the elements and the origins of his profound and penetrating researches, yet using besides the most admirable logical power in working out his conceptions. In addition to his brilliant inventive genius we must recognize in him an ability for the finest and most fruitful generalizations of mathematical relations, which has often enabled him to push back, far beyond the point where others have hitherto been stopped, the limits of our knowledge in different branches of pure and applied mathematics. This was shown already in his first work on automorphic functions with which he began the series of his brilliant publications which must be classed with the greatest mathematical discoveries of all time."

In this country Poincaré has become known largely through the efforts of Professor George Bruce Halsted of the State Normal School of Greeley, Colorado, who has translated his philosophical works and has for many years been indefatigable in spreading the new gospel of the non-Euclidian geometry. Professor Halsted has at my request kindly contributed the following account of one of Poincaré's astronomical triumphs and of the visit that Professor Sylvester of Johns Hopkins paid to Poincaré many years ago:

"The kernel of Poincaré's power lies in an oracle Sylvester often quoted from Hesiod: Only the genius knows how much more the part is than the whole. He penetrates at once the divine simplicity of the perfectly general case, and thence descends, as from Olympus, to the special concrete earthly particulars. Thus his memoir of 1885, which Sir George Darwin says came to him as a revelation, on a rotating fluid mass, and his book 'Les Méthodes nouvelles de la Mécanique céleste,' 1892–1899, were ready with prevision when the shocking special case occurred of Phœbe, ninth satellite of Saturn, discovered in

1900, afterward found, incredible as it seemed, to be revolving in the direction contrary to that of all the others. It follows that Saturn himself originally rotated in the reverse direction. Again, on February 29, 1908, was found an eighth satellite of Jupiter, Jviii, revolving round Jove in the shocking Phœbe retrograde direction. Zeus must have turned over. All the planets have turned over, and some are now making another somersault. Moreover, Jviii does not even revolve in a closed orbit; its path is an open twister of unreturning turns.

"For Poincaré the inexhaustible source, the lamp of Aladdin, has ever been the non-Euclidian geometry. In him the Bolyai-Lobachevski-Riemann germ flowers fair.

"Personally Poincaré is the most lovable of men. At our very first meeting I realized that I had already been intimately associated with him for two years in the person of Sylvester. I told him the story of Sylvester's discovery of him, and he showed me how vividly and tenderly reconnaissant he was toward the great old master.

"Midsummer, and up a stuffy Paris stairway labors a giant gnome, beard on enormous chest, fortunately no neck, for no neck could upbear such a monstrous head, bald but for the inverted halo of hair collaring its juncture with the broad shoulders; small inefficient hands holding big hat and damp handkerchief; breath puffing with the heat and exertion. It is Sylvester, self-driven to seek out the source of new creations strangely akin to his own. At the sought door, open, he pauses, seized by doubt, the person within is so young, so slight, so dazed. Can this be the new incarnation of the eternal world-genius of geometry? But the aloof sensitiveness of the face, the broad sphericity of the head reassure him. This is Henri Poincaré. And so the old King finds the True Prince, who in turn finds himself at last truly comprehended, anointed to the succession, and given high heart to establish his dominion."

The sudden death of Henri Poincaré, July 18, 1912, at the age of fifty-eight, shocked the scientific world. This marvelous thinking machine was stopped, this repository of the exact sciences was lost to the world, by the trifling accident of a clot of blood catching in one of the valves of the heart. He had gone to the hospital for a minor operation which was apparently successful. Ten days later he was pronounced well enough to leave and was dressing when he was struck down.

The funeral service at the church of Saint-Jacques-du-Haut-Pas was attended by a remarkable assemblage of men of science and letters, government officials, and representatives of foreign countries. At the Montparnasse cemetery orations were delivered by M. Guist'hau, Minister of Public Instruction, Jules Claretie of the Académie française, M. Appell, dean of the Faculty of Sciences, M. Bigourdan of the Observatory, Paul Painlevé of the Academy of Sciences, and General Cornille, Commandant of the École polytechnique. M. Painlevé said of him:

"The life of Henri Poincaré was one intense and uninterrupted meditation, that despotic and pitiless meditation which bows the shoulders and bends the head, which absorbs the vital influx of one's being and too soon uses up the body it possesses.

"Henri Poincaré was not only a great creator in the positive sciences; he was a great philosopher and a great writer. Certain of his aphorisms remind one of Pascal: 'Thought is only a flash between two long nights, but this flash is everything.' His style followed the movement of his thought; brief and arresting formulas, often paradoxical when isolated, joined by hasty explanations which discard the easy details and say only the essential. This is why superficial critics have accused him of being 'incoherent'; the truth being that without some previous scientific education, such logical movement is difficult to follow. Mice cannot keep step with a lion.

" It is likewise a lack of comprehension of his philosophy as a whole that has led certain commentators to think they found a transcendental skepticism in his critical studies of the principles of science. Must he not have had faith in science who has written 'The search for truth ought to be the aim of our activity; it is the sole aim worthy of it'? His philosophy of the rational science will live as long as his own discoveries. The totality of the mathematical sciences seemed to him like a gigantic measuring instrument, harmoniously adjusted and well adapted for the evaluation of the phenomena of the universe. There remains one trait of his character that I cannot pass over in silence; that is his admirable intellectual sincerity. He gave himself, he gave to all, so far as words permit, the whole of his thought and even the mechanism of his thought. In his last publication, appearing only a few days before his death and dealing with the problem of the stability of our universe, he excused himself for giving out such incomplete results:

"'It would seem under these conditions that I ought to abstain from all publication until I had solved the problem, but after the fruitless efforts I have made for months, it appeared to me wisest to let the problem ripen while I let it alone for some years. That would have been very well if I had been sure of taking it up again some day, *but at my age I could not be sure of that.* Besides, the importance of the subject is too great, and the results already obtained are on the whole too considerable for me to be content to leave them altogether useless. I hope that the geometricians who will interest themselves in this problem and who will doubtless be more fortunate than I will be able to get something out of it and make use of it in finding the path they should pursue.'

" What words can be added to this scientific testament, so simple and so noble, of a life altogether consecrated, without faltering even to the last hour, to the search for truth ? For the first time in half a century this unparalleled brain has found repose."

Poincaré, as we have seen, was awake to the wider aspects of science. He was interested in its effects upon human life and conduct, although he himself was engaged in one of its most remote and abstract branches. Shortly before his death he discussed a question which nowadays arouses intense interest, the question of what effect the advance and popularization of science will have on ethics. Will science in destroying superstitions, in changing utterly the traditional way of regarding the universe

and man, undermine the morality which forms the
foundation of our civilization ? This question Poincaré answers in the negative. He believes that our
moral instincts lie too deep to be affected by such
a revolution in thought, but on the other hand he
does not think, as some do, that science will ever
be able of itself to provide the moral imperative.
A few paragraphs from this essay, published post-
humously in "Last Thoughts", may well serve as
a conclusion to this sketch of his philosophy :

> There can be no scientific morality ; but no more
> can there be immoral science. And the reason is
> simple ; it is a reason — how shall I say it ? — purely
> grammatical.
> If the premises of a syllogism are both in the
> indicative, the conclusion likewise will be in the
> indicative. For the conclusion to be put in the im-
> perative, it would be necessary that at least one of
> the premises should itself be in the imperative.
> Now, the principles of science, the postulates of
> geometry, are and can be only in the indicative ; still
> in this same mood are the experimental verities,
> and at the foundation of the sciences there is, there
> can be, nothing else. Hence, the most subtle dialec-
> tician may juggle with these principles as he will,
> combine them, frame them up one upon another ;
> all he will get from them will be in the indicative.
> He will never obtain a proposition which shall say :
> do this, or don't do that ; that is to say, a proposition
> which confirms or contradicts morality. . . .
> Some therefore think that science will be destruc-

tive; they fear the ruin it will make and dread lest, where it shall have passed, society can no longer survive.

Is there not in these fears a sort of internal contradiction? If it is scientifically proved that such or such a custom, regarded as indispensable to the very existence of human society, had not in reality the importance attributed to it and deceived us only by its venerable antiquity, if that be proved, admitting this proof to be possible, will the moral life of humanity be shaken? One of two things, either this custom is useful, and then a reasonable science cannot prove that it is not; or else it is useless and we should not regret it. From the moment that we place at the foundation of our syllogisms one of those generous emotions which engender morality, it is still this emotion, and consequently it is still morality which we must find at the end of our whole chain of reasonings, if this has been conducted in accordance with the rules of logic. What is in danger of perishing is the non-essential, that which was merely an accident in our moral life; the sole important thing cannot fail to be found in the conclusions since it is in the premises. . . .

Science, right or wrong, is deterministic; everywhere it penetrates it introduces determinism. So long as it is only a question of physics or even of biology, this is unimportant. The domain of conscience remains inviolate. What will happen when morality in turn shall become the object of science?

Is all despair, or if some day morality should accommodate itself to determinism, could it so adapt itself without dying from the effects? So profound a metaphysical revolution would doubtless have much less influence upon morals than we think.

HENRI POINCARÉ

It is of course understood that penal repression is not in question. What is called crime or punishment, would be called sickness or prophylaxis, but society would retain intact its right, which is not to punish, but simply the right of self-defense. What is more serious is that the idea of merit or demerit would have to disappear or be transformed. But we should continue to love the good man, as we love all that is beautiful; we should no longer have the right to hate the vicious man, who would then inspire only disgust; but is hate necessary? Enough that we do not cease to hate vice.

Apart from that, all would go on as in the past. Instinct is stronger than all metaphysics, and even though one should have laid it bare, even if one should understand the secret of its force, its power would not thereby be weakened. Is gravitation less irresistible since Newton? The moral forces which guide us would continue to guide us.[1]

How to Read Poincaré

A complete analytical bibliography of Poincaré's writings up to 1909 will be found in Ernest Lebon's "Henri Poincaré" (Paris: Gaultier-Villars), which contains the biographical address of M. Frédéric Masson on his admission to the French Academy and other eulogies. The list comprises 436 articles and books classified as follows: Mathematical analysis, 146; analytical and celestial mechanics,

[1] Translated by Professor Halsted from "Science and Morals" in *Dernières Pensées*.

85; mathematic physics, 78; scientific philosophy, 51; necrology, 17; miscellaneous, 59; an astonishing output for thirty years' work, considering the amount and difficulty of the labor involved in some of the contributions.

The mathematical works of Poincaré are too difficult for the layman and indeed for many professional mathematicians. But there are five volumes of general interest published by Flammarion, Paris: "La Science et l'Hypothèse", "La Valeur de la Science", "Science et Méthode", "Savants et Ecrivains", and "Dernières Pensées." The first of these has had a wide popularity, having been translated into English, German, Spanish, Hungarian, and Japanese. The English translation of "Science and Hypothesis", by Professor George Bruce Halsted (New York: Science Press), which appeared in 1905, is introduced by an interesting criticism of Poincaré's philosophy by Professor Josiah Royce, of Harvard. Two years later "The Value of Science" was published in this country (Science Press). "Science et Méthode", though it contains some matter of more general interest than the others, particularly his account of the rôle played by unconscious mind in mathematical invention and his explanation of the newer conceptions of physics, has not yet appeared in English. The fourth volume, "Savants et Ecrivains", is an evidence of Poincaré's good will rather than his literary talents, as it consists of perfunctory addresses on deceased Academicians, the most extensive being that on Sully-Prudhomme, whose chair he holds. The fifth, published after his death, contains the essay on "Science and Morality" from which I have quoted, as well as interesting discussions of recent science and philosophy. The volume entitled "Foundations of Science" (published by the Science Press, New York) contains "Science and Hypothesis", "Value of Science", and "Science and Method" with the introduction by Professor Royce.

From either of the two volumes, "Science and Hypothesis" or "The Value of Science", one can get an idea of Poincaré's philosophy, which is of importance because it is not merely the philosophy of an individual but the point of view of most men of science nowadays, though rarely so definitely recognized or clearly expressed. Both books consist of a somewhat heterogeneous collection of studies on the method and logic of the mathematical and physical sciences, containing much that the general reader will have to skip because of its use of unfamiliar terms, but it will not be safe for him to skip any whole pages without looking them over carefully, for he is likely to find brilliant and suggestive sentences embedded in the most unpromising material.

Separate articles by Poincaré, forming chapters from the above-mentioned volumes, are accessible in American periodicals. "The Future of Mathematics" in *Monist*, Vol. XX, pp. 76–92; also in the 1909 Smithsonian Report, which is in every public library. "The Choice of Facts" in *Monist*, Vol. XIX, pp. 231–239. "The Principles of Mathematical Physics" in the report of the St. Louis Congress of Arts and Sciences, Vol. I, pp. 604–624, and in *Monist*, Vol. XV, pp. 1–24. "The Bolyai Prize" (Report on the Work of Hilbert) in *Science*, May 19 and 26, 1911. "Mathematical Creations" in *Monist*, Vol. XX, pp. 321–335. "The Value of Science" was first published complete in the *Popular Science Monthly*, September, 1906, and later;

"Relativity of Space", "The New Logics", and "Chance" in the *Monist*, 1913.

For biographical details besides the references already given in footnotes, see Nordmann's article on Poincaré in Smithsonian Report, 1912; Darbou's eulogy in *Le Temps*, December 15, 1913; and articles in *Revue du Mois*, February 10, 1913; *La Revue de Paris*, February 15, 1913; *The Nation*, September 12, 1912.

CHAPTER IV

ÉLIE METCHNIKOFF

Ever since the attempt has been made to discover a rational basis of morality, human nature, regarded essentially as good, has been taken as that basis. Religions and systems of philosophy, on the other hand, which have tried to find another foundation for morality, have regarded human nature as vicious at the roots. Science has been able to tell us that man, the descendant of animals, has good and evil qualities in his nature, and that his life is made unhappy by the evil qualities. But the constitution of man is not immutable, and perhaps it may be changed for the better.

Morality should be based not on human nature in its existing vitiated condition, but on human nature, ideal, as it may be in the future. Before all things, it is necessary to try to amend the evolution of the human life, that is to say, to transform its disharmonies into harmonies (Orthobiosis). This task can be undertaken only by science, and to science the opportunity of accomplishing it must be given. — Metchnikoff's "The Nature of Man", p. 288.

If Carlyle were writing now his "Heroes and Hero-Worship", he would have to add — however much he would have disliked to — a chapter on "The

Hero as Scientist." For the popular ideal of greatness has been decidedly changed in the last half-
century, and new standards of heroism have been
established. Creative genius is beginning to take
rank above destructive, and men are coming to
recognize that the heroism of those who save life
may be quite as great and is certainly more admirable than the heroism that is measured by a monument of skulls. A striking proof of this shifting
of public appreciation is afforded by the referendum
carried out by the *Petit Parisien* a few years ago to
ascertain whom the French people regarded as the
greatest names their country had produced during
the nineteenth century. Fifteen million answers
were sent in, so the result may be taken as repre-
senting the consensus of opinion in a larger degree
than such newspaper *plébiscites* generally do. It
was to be expected that the name of Napoleon
would head such a list. It would have in almost
any other country except France. But France,
always devoted to the cult of *La Gloire* and hitherto
chiefly captivated by the bellicose form of it ; France,
where every man is trained in the army and educated
in schools established with the avowed purpose of
increasing the military strength of the nation ;
France ranks Napoleon fourth in the list of eminent

men and puts at the head of it the name of a modest
chemist and physiologist, Louis Pasteur.[1] It is
a common observation that new ideas and social
tendencies are apt to become manifest in France
earlier than elsewhere. The French clock seems
to be fast, always keeping a bit ahead of mean
European time. If so, we may expect that before
long other countries may come to give due honor
and, what is more important, due opportunity and
encouragement to the scientists, inventors, and
authors who confer glory upon their country by
benefiting the whole world.

[1] The list is instructive because it shows clearly that the names first
in the hearts of their countrymen are those who have become eminent in
science and letters or have done signal service in the cause of the republic.
The leading names are as follows: 1, Pasteur (receiving 1,338,425 votes);
2, Victor Hugo (1,227,103); 3, Gambetta (1,155,672); 4, Napoleon
Bonaparte (1,118,034); 5, Thiers (1,039,453); 6, Lazare Carnot, organ-
izer of the republican army of the Revolution; 7, Pierre Curie, discoverer
of radium; 8, Alexandre Dumas, *père;* 9, Dr. Roux, inventor of the
diphtheritic serum; 10, Parmentier, introducer of the potato into
France; 11, Ampère, father of dynamic electricity; 12, Brazza, who
secured the Kongo region for France; 13, Zola, novelist and defender of
Dreyfus; 14, Lamartine, republican poet; 15, Arago, astronomer and
physicist; 16, Sarah Bernhardt, actress; 17, Premier Waldeck-Rousseau;
18, Marshal MacMahon; 19, President Carnot; 20, Chevreul, chemist;
21, Chateaubriand; 22, Ferdinand de Lesseps, constructor of the Suez
Canal and projector of the Panama; 23, Michelet; 24, Jacquard, inventor of the pattern loom; 25, Jules Verne; 26, President Loubet;
27, Deufert-Rochereau, defender of Belfort.

The worthy successor of Pasteur as Director of the Institute he founded is the subject of this sketch, Élie Metchnikoff. The foremost of French medical men, he was neither born a Frenchman nor trained as a physician. Like Pasteur, he entered the realm of medicine by crossing the frontier of another science. Any man who pursues a straight line of thought will find that it leads him across many of those imaginary lines which have been drawn between the sciences, just as an aviator crossing Europe in an air line pays no attention to the artificial and historic boundaries which divide state from state. Pasteur was a chemist, an inorganic chemist at that, and he was running down the cause of asymmetry in crystals when he found himself over in the field of biology. He had been engaged in separating the leftward skewed crystals of tartaric acid from those that skewed to the right by picking them out of the mixture by hand, but he discovered that he could throw the burden of selection off on an agency whose time was less valuable, namely, the yeast plant, which has an appetite for one kind of crystals, but disdains the other. This led him to the germ theory of life and of disease and enabled him to save millions annually to the farmer and stockraiser and unnumbered human lives.

Mr. Merezhkosh.

ÉLIE METCHNIKOFF

Metchnikoff's experience was similar. He was as a zoölogist less interested in man than in the invertebrates, devoting his time to the study of the minuter forms of life on the barren steppes of Russia and in Mediterranean waters. It was in Italy at Messina in 1882 that he made the discovery which led him to fame as one of the benefactors of the human race. Now, if a man should deliberately set out for such a goal, if he should be incited by egotism to become famous, or inspired by altruism to relieve the suffering of humanity, about the last thing he would try would be to sit down in a laboratory all day with his eye glued to a microscope watching the blood corpuscles chase each other through the veins of an infant starfish. But since Metchnikoff was less influenced by the two motives mentioned than he was by a desire for truth for its own sake and regardless of consequences, all these things have been added unto him. If the anti-vivisectionists had their way about it, experimentation in animals, if allowed at all, would be restricted to physicians and to the specific purpose of curing disease. This, however, would be one of the surest ways to check medical progress, for the advancement of a science ordinarily owes little to those who are professionally engaged in its practice or have their eyes focused

[151]

upon some practical result of their investigations. At least the world may rejoice that through the liberality of French law the work of these two men has never been hampered — Pasteur, who discovered the cause of disease, and Metchnikoff, who discovered the cause of immunity. These are two cornerstones of the foundation on which is now being erected the structure of a rational system of hygiene the purpose of which is to prolong human life by the elimination of disease rather than by its cure. The change that is taking place in medicine is analogous to that taking place in philanthropy. The modern philanthropist appears cold-hearted because, instead of dropping a coin into a beggar's hat, as did the charitable in former days, he devotes himself to a systematic study of the causes of poverty. The modern medical man is likewise misunderstood if he seems indifferent to the suffering around him and is absorbed in the investigation of remote biological problems having no perceptible relation to human needs. But the beneficial results of the scientific method in both philanthropy and medicine are already sufficiently apparent to enable us to see that it will do much more for humanity than the kind but blind benevolence of the past.

The fame of France in art, literature, and science

is in large part her reward for her hospitality in giving to men of other lands the freedom and encouragement which they could not find at home. One example is Maeterlinck. Another is Metchnikoff. He left his native country chiefly because of a difference of opinion on political questions between himself and the Czar. Not that he has ever been a revolutionist, but as a Jew by race, an atheist in religion, and a liberal in politics, he was triply obnoxious to the powers that be, and after the assassination of Alexander II in 1881, the students were too much excited over politics to attend to their studies. So he resigned his professorship in the University of Odessa and went abroad to devote himself to biological research.

He was born in the Province of Kharkov, Little Russia, May 15, 1845. His father was an officer of the Guards, afterward a general. His mother was a Jewess, and it was from her that he derived the love for science which early manifested itself. He won a gold medal in the high school of Kharkov and passed through the university of that city in two years instead of the customary four. Then he went to Germany and studied at Giessen, Göttingen, and Munich. Returning to his native land, he taught in the University of St. Petersburg and in 1870 went to Odessa to take the chair of zoölogy in the university there.

The years spent in private study, chiefly at Messina, the earthquake city of Sicily, were most fruitful, for his investigation of intercellular digestion in minute marine invertebrates gave him the clew to the protective action of the blood in the higher animals and man, and in 1884 he outlined his theory of inflammation, which was, in short, that the congestion of blood at a wound was due to the efforts of the leucocytes or white blood cells to overpower the invading microbes. The value of this discovery was recognized immediately by the two foremost authorities in biology : Virchow, the German, who had discovered the leucocytes, and Pasteur, the Frenchman, who had discovered the microbes. Metchnikoff had now found the missing link which brought these two discoveries together and showed their meaning.

In 1888 Metchnikoff was called to the Pasteur Institute, and in 1895 became its director. Here he found an exceptional opportunity to devote his talents to the relief of suffering humanity. Such institutions for the advancement of the science of medicine have since been established elsewhere : the Institute for Experimental Therapeutics in

ÉLIE METCHNIKOFF

Frankfort-on-the-Main, the Cancer Research Laboratory of London, the Rockefeller Institute in New York, for example; but the French people were the first to respond to the need of the man they have delighted to honor by endowing, in 1886, an institution which should continue his work as well as perpetuate his name. The Nobel prize for the most important discovery in medicine was in 1908 divided between Metchnikoff, of the Pasteur Institute, and Professor Paul Ehrlich, of the Frankfort Institute, who has in these latter days made "606" the mark of the beast, instead of 666, as prophesied in Revelation. The Nobel prize man of 1912, Doctor Alexis Carrel, although a Frenchman by birth, found in the Rockefeller Institute the opportunity to carry on his remarkable investigations on the preservation and transplantation of living tissues.

Characteristically French is the artistic setting which has been given to this home of science. The visitor appropriately approaches it through the long and handsome Boulevard Pasteur, then turning into a side street he finds on his left the Pasteur Institute and on his right the more imposing buildings of the Institute for Infectious Diseases and the Laboratory of Biological Chemistry, recently erected for carrying out the treatment which the experimental work of the other side of the street has suggested. A new department has been added for the study of tropical diseases such as the sleeping sickness, which has depopulated a large part of the Nyanza region. This extension of the work is made possible by the receipt in 1909 of the bequest of eight million dollars by the miserly and eccentric Jewish banker who called himself Osiris.

As the visitor passes into the courtyard of the Institute, his nerves already shaky with thoughts of microbes and mad dogs, he is almost startled to see, half hidden among the trees, a man engaged in a death struggle with a wolf. This is a bronze statue of Jupile, a shepherd who, bitten by a mad wolf, was one of the first patients to receive the Pasteur treatment for rabies. In a crypt of marble and mosaic underneath the building is the tomb of Pasteur, as impressive, if less imposing, than the tomb of Napoleon under the dome of the Invalides not far away. The reception room of the Institute is adorned with large paintings showing the modern miracles of healing, better authenticated than those of Sainte Geneviève depicted by Puvis de Chavannes on the walls of the Panthéon.

Professor Metchnikoff is ordinarily not accessible to visitors, especially interviewers, but since I was armed with a letter of introduction from Professor Jacques Loeb, of the Rockefeller Institute, whom he regards as the foremost of American scientists, I was fortunate enough to find him in.

He has rather a short figure and a large head, with a bushy gray beard, but hair that is still dark. His spectacles are not sufficient to impart severity to his mild blue eyes. His voice is low and pleasant, and he speaks, as he moves, without either hurry or hesitation. He is a worker among workers, inspiring with his indefatigable zeal the young men who come to him from Europe, America, and Asia to pursue their researches in bacteriology.

A walk through the Pasteur Institute is like a visit to a zoölogical garden, for the study of each particular human disease requires the discovery of some species that is also susceptible to it. Here are not only the dogs, guinea pigs, and rats common to every bacteriological laboratory, but also many others closely connected with Metchnikoff's special interests; parrots and geese, for example, which are remarkable for their longevity; bats, which eat rotten food and yet maintain an aseptic intestinal tract; and chimpanzees, which, as the literal blood relations of man, are capable of sharing the worst of his diseases.

Like Agassiz, Metchnikoff has "no time to get rich." At his home in the suburbs of Paris he sets an example of the plain living he advocates, supplementing the meager salary given him at the Institute by the income of a small estate in Russia. The twenty thousand dollars he received from the Nobel Foundation he devoted entirely to the furtherance of his researches in longevity.

M. Metchnikoff has given the best possible proof that he has no personal aversion to women who enter his profession, for he married in 1875 as his second wife a Russian bacteriologist of distinction. He dedicated to her his first volume of "Optimistic Studies," and in it he cites her experiments on the growth of microbe-free tadpoles. She is an artist as well as a scientist, and here, too, M. Metchnikoff shares her tastes, for he is fond of painting and music. They have no children, but he has a godchild to whom he is devoted.

His high regard for individuality leads him to look with favor upon the entrance of women into the universities and the professions. He has no fear that it will result in the production of a class of celibates corresponding to the sexless workers of the beehive. On the contrary, his observation of the feminist movement for more than forty years has shown him that learned ladies are by no means wanting in the marital and maternal instincts common and proper to their sex. Of a thousand women in the St. Petersburg Medical School, ten per cent had been married before, and forty-four per cent were married during their course of study. A conspicuous case of feminine scientific genius is that of Sonya Kovalevsky, who attained the highest eminence in that field which, by the common consent of men, was formerly regarded as unattainable by women; that is, pure mathematics. But the day when she received the doubled prize of the French Academy of Sciences she wrote to a friend that she had never felt so unhappy, and the cause of her unhappiness, as revealed in her letters and romances, was that she was not beloved as other women were.

Although Metchnikoff would grant to women every opportunity for the exercise of their talents, and thinks they had better occupy themselves with science than with fashions, he believes genius of a high order to be much rarer among them than among men. When he was called upon by the women doctors and scientists at the Naturalists' Congress at St. Petersburg for his opinion of the feminist movement, he created considerable con-

sternation among them by the following frank
language :

Your complaint, as I understand it, is that man
has excluded woman from all higher intellectual
occupation by unnatural means, so that her mind has
become atrophied, her capabilities blunted, her
talents stagnant. You would remedy all this by
being made man's equal in politics. You would
then, you say, develop your slumbering abilities,
overtake, and possibly surpass, your immemorial
enslaver — man.

But do you really need this political equality in
order to attain this supremacy ? Has the down-
trodden among men ever needed it ? His political
equality has come as an effect not as the cause of his
intellectual development. The mind that dominates in the artistic and scientific world ultimately
arrives at political supremacy.

But what art or science has man closed to you ?
You are here ; but really, ladies, I have failed to
discover a Bichat, a Louis, a Jenner, or a Pasteur
among you. Have you personally been impeded in
your careers more than certain individuals among
men ? Now let us take the arts. Is there a man-
master so unnatural who ever forbade his female
slave to express herself in music ? But where are
your Beethovens, your Wagners, your Verdis, your
Brahms ? I beg of you, dear ladies, if you remember
one, tell me.

What brutal slave owner at any time forbade
women to beautify canvas with satisfying hues and
lines depicting life or nature ? As in music, man has
encouraged women to do these things, yet where are
your Raphaels, your Leonardos, your Rubenses ?

ÉLIE METCHNIKOFF,

Have women been forbidden to mold, carve, or draw ? Yet where is your Phidias, your Michelangelo, your Cellini ? Did you ever hear of a woman architect ?

Home and motherhood there, of course, the most radical among you will not say that man has attempted to restrain you — there you have had from time immemorial, in all ages, in all places, under every condition, absolute and full freedom. Still, is it not man, the enslaver, who teaches you domestic economy ? Is it not from man that you have learned how to care for your offspring in illness, how to amuse them in health ? Who discovered the laws of domestic hygiene ? Was it a woman ?

Now, my dear ladies, has man ever excluded you from the kitchen ? No, you say, you have been enslaved there. "Cook! Feed the brute!" is eternally dinned in your ears. It would seem reasonable that at least in this sphere woman should have reached a high standard of perfection. And the actual result ? Ah, dear ladies, I must confess. If I want a really good dinner I must have recourse to a chef.

And now, ladies, I ask your pardon, you have all studied physiology and psychology, and you know where such considerations would lead me. But one word more : Do not lose sight of the significance of your request, "Professor, what is your opinion of the feministic movement ?" for that makes out your case perfectly — to advocate your cause you would call in the help of man.

Metchnikoff has very little liking for the political methods in vogue in our republics. He thinks young men too reckless, opinionated, and pessimistic to be intrusted with the ballot at the age of twenty-one. "It is easily intelligible," he says, "that in the new conditions such modern idols as universal suffrage, public opinion, and the referendum, in which the ignorant masses are called upon to decide questions which demand varied and profound knowledge, will last no longer than the old idols. The progress of human knowledge will bring about the replacement of such institutions by others in which applied morality will be controlled by really competent persons." But he fails to inform us how these "competent persons" are to be selected and placed in power.

To give an account of the varied researches which Metchnikoff has carried on or has superintended at the Pasteur Institute is apart from our purpose and would in any case be impossible here, because it would involve the recapitulation of a great part of the history of medical progress for the past quarter century. During this period the science of medicine has been completely revolutionized, for the use of traditional and empirical remedies has been largely replaced by a systematic search for the causes of diseases and the experimental determination of methods of avoiding or counteracting them. In general, the change may be characterized as a return to nature. In the older medicine at its best, a dose of some vegetable or mineral substance, such as quinine or mercury, comparatively harmless, but altogether foreign to the body, was administered through the mouth and in time reaching the blood through the digestive systems, killed off or paralyzed the disease germ. In modern medicine at its best, some substance, such as the diphtheria antitoxin, that is already present in the blood in quantity sufficient under ordinary circumstances to prevent infection, is reënforced in an emergency by more of the same substance prepared in the blood of the horse. Or if that cannot be done, the next best thing is to inject some serum that by a natural reaction will stimulate the body to prepare in excess its own antitoxin or excite the phagocytes to greater exertions in overcoming their enemies. In any case, the object is to induce an artificial immunity as nearly as possible like the natural immunity of the healthy body.

Phagocytes — that is, "devouring cells" — was the name given by Metchnikoff to the leucocytes or white cells, which he found wandering about the body in search of their prey. They lead a sort of semi-independent life, like the simplest one-celled animal, the amœba, and they penetrate to all parts

of the body, even squeezing in between the toughened
tissue of the skin and bones. When a cut is made
in the skin they are borne to the breach by the flow
of blood and there pile up and coagulate, forming
a new skin to protect the raw flesh, somewhat as
a breach in a rampart is hastily filled in with sand
bags. Not only that, but when the enemy actually
gains entrance either by storming a wound or sneak-
ing in through some unguarded opening, then the
white cells rally to the attack, surrounding and destroying the invading microbes. If these multiply
too rapidly, the phagocyte reserves are mobilized,
new recruits by the million are called out, until
the bodily force is victorious or exhausted. Such
a battle we call a local inflammation, or, if the en-
gagement is general and long continued, a fever.
Under the microscope we may watch the foes engaged in single combat, the phagocyte devouring the bacillus, a living, formless mass of protoplasm,
stretching out extemporized tentacles and engulfing
the rod, globe, or writhing spiral which we may
afterward see slowly digesting in its interior.

To be sure, the operation is not quite so simple
as Metchnikoff first conceived it. A condition is
always more complicated than the theory devised
to explain it. The question has been hotly debated

and is not yet settled whether the phagocytes best defend us by their life or by their death. It appears that as they undergo dissolution they give up to the blood certain substances which dissolve the disease germs or neutralize their poisons, and this may be a more important means of defense than the englobing or engulfing process. Then, too, these white cells seem at times strangely indifferent to the presence of their dearest foes, or, perhaps we should say, their favorite food. There is needed in the blood on such occasions a substance known as opsonin, which being absorbed by the microbes the phagocytes attack them with avidity; this opsonin serving as some biologist, doubtless an Englishman, has said, like Worcestershire sauce as an appetizer to the phagocytes.

But for further discussion of these questions I must refer the reader to his family physician, who will take pleasure in repudiating these vague and fanciful interpretations of mine. He will be able to tell whether phagocytosis or bacteriolysis is the fashionable mode of combating disease germs and he will introduce the reader to alexin, agglutinin, anti-bodies, sidechains, and other interesting and useful novelties that he contains within him to a greater or less degree, let us hope a greater.

But these same voracious white blood cells which ordinarily serve as the defenders of the body may in the period of its weakness become its worst enemies. This reminds us of the Prætorian Guards who in the later days of Rome precipitated its decline by attacking the capital. The phagocytes show an unfortunate predilection for the higher elements of the human organism and, according to Metchnikoff, the most distressing symptom of old age, the weakening of the mind, is due to their devouring the nerve cells. But besides that they play havoc all through the body; eating up the pigment of the hair and so whitening it; causing degeneration of the liver and kidneys; robbing the skeleton of its lime and depositing it in the blood vessels, thus doing double damage by weakening the bones and hardening the arteries. In these symptoms of senility the germs of disease form an important factor, both in weakening the body and instigating the treacherous insurrection of the phagocytes. Hence Metchnikoff comes to the conclusion that: "The senile degeneration of an organism is entirely similar to the lesions induced by certain maladies of a microbic origin", and thus he arrives at his famous definition: "Old age is an infectious chronic disease, characterized by a degeneration or an enfeebling of the noble elements and by the excessive activity of the phagocytes."

If old age is correctly characterized as a disease, and especially if it is due in part to microbic invasion, it ought to be possible to cure or postpone it. This, then, is what Metchnikoff has in recent years made the main aim of his researches.

In particular he suspects the large intestine of harboring some of the most dangerous of the microscopic enemies of man, the cause of many of the ills that flesh is heir to. It is in his opinion an excessive and comparatively unimportant organ, for it can be shortened or removed without serious consequences. A comparative survey of the anatomy of the vertebrates shows that as a general rule the longer the intestine the shorter the life. He does not advocate its extirpation by surgery or its disinfection by chemicals, but he would crowd out its wild and poisonous flora by harmless cultivated species. Among the friendly microbes he regards the lactic acid bacilli as most useful for this purpose. These act upon milk or fruit sugar, converting it into lactic acid, which is destructive to most other microbes, including some of the most dangerous. For example, mysterious outbreaks of typhoid fever have been recently traced to "typhoid carriers"; that is, persons who, while immune to the disease themselves, may yet serve for years as conveyors of the infection. But a thriving colony of Bulgarian bacilli will drive out the typhoid bacilli and so put a stop to the spread of the disease.

The difference between harmless and injurious bacteria on which the lactic acid theory depends is easily understood because it is a matter of common observation. Meat and milk have much the same composition so far as their protein is concerned. But whereas meat promptly spoils, that is, putrefies, with the formation of disgusting and poisonous products of decomposition, milk sours instead and will remain wholesome and to some tastes palatable for several days. Both are the results of bacterial decomposition, but the difference is due to the fact that milk contains a kind of sugar which, inoculated with the proper bacilli, is converted into lactic acid, and thus the growth of the bacteria of putrefaction is for some time prevented. But under certain circumstances it happens that the latter get the start of the lactic acid makers, and then the milk goes the way of the meat, and we have a case of "ptomain poisoning." In short, the aim of swallowing cultures of lactic acid bacilli by wholesale is to keep the contents of the remote regions of our digestive apparatus in the condition of soured milk rather than that of decayed meat. Recently the same treatment has been recommended for preserving the teeth, since these mild-mannered and beneficent bacilli rubbed into the gums will dispossess those which ordinarily grow in our mouths and attack our teeth.

For aid in his fight against the bacterial poisons that bring on disease and old age, Metchnikoff has resorted to his native steppes. The Tartars and Kalmucks of southern Russia had always had as their favorite food koumiss, prepared by the fermentation of mare's milk, and nomads of all races have made use of some form of curdled milk, chiefly because of the difficulty of preserving other kinds of animal food under primitive conditions. The keffir of the Caucasus, the leben of Egypt, the matzoon of Armenia, the dadhi of India, and yahourth of Bulgaria are all produced from milk by the use of various species of lactic acid bacilli associated with other bacteria of fermentation. Of these the last, the Bulgarian yahourth, yoghourt, or yagurt, contains the strongest bacilli; that is, those that are able to stand the largest percentage of the product of their own activity, lactic acid, and so Metchnikoff has made them the basis of his dietetics.

A surprisingly large proportion of centenarians
are reported from Bulgaria, where yagurt is used,
and Metchnikoff cites a large number of cases of
men and women of extreme old age who have lived
largely on sour milk or on sauerkraut, which also
contains the lactic acid bacilli.[1] Most of these
are found among the poorer classes or comparatively uncivilized races. Sir Moses Montefiore
is one of the very few rich men who have passed the
century mark. Metchnikoff uses this as an argument for the simple life. But it is questionable
whether such data, derived from the casual reports
of individual cases and the generalized observations
of travelers, are of much evidential value. Claims
to longevity among the unlettered are notoriously
unreliable. It would be very unsafe to hold that
the negroes were longer lived than the whites, because so many mammies could tell of remembering
Washington. When the British old age pension
bill passed, the number of poor people in Ireland
who came forward with evidence that they were
over sixty-five years old surprised the actuaries

---

[1] He might add to his notable examples of persons addicted to the use
of curdled milk the case of Tze-Hsi, the Dowager Empress of China, who
at the age of seventy-four had energy enough to change her own mind
and revolutionize the government of four hundred million people.

and embarrassed the budget. Women are apt to restore double-fold in old age the years they deprived themselves of in the later thirties.

It is also curious to see a skeptic like Metchnikoff giving serious consideration to the accounts of longevity given in the Pentateuch which many orthodox theologians are willing to concede as legendary. He balks, indeed, at Noah's nine hundred and fifty years and Methuselah's nine hundred and sixty-nine, but accepts as probable Aaron's one hundred and twenty-three years and Moses's one hundred and twenty, quoting the words of Jehovah: "My spirit shall not always strive with man for that he also is flesh; yet his days shall be an hundred and twenty years." He accounts for it by their more healthful mode of living and their freedom from alcoholism and the diseases of vice, nowadays the chief cause of premature old age. He calls attention also to the fact that sour milk was in common use among the patriarchs and was esteemed by Abraham food fit to set before angels. In regard to the Mosaic dietary regulations he says:

Some of them, it is true, such as the prohibition of uncooked or partially cooked meat, are confirmed by modern knowledge. But the greater number of the Mosaic rules, as, for instance, the prohibition of the consumption as food of blood or the flesh of pigs or hares, and so forth, are in direct opposition to a modern knowledge of hygienic diet.

Metchnikoff, being a scientist, uses, of course, these reports of longevity gathered from historians and travelers merely as suggesting profitable lines of research, not as proof of any theory. Such proof can only be obtained by direct experimentation, and accordingly he has for the past fifteen years been experimenting upon himself. The Pasteur people do not belong to that class of physicians who refuse to take their own medicine. Metchnikoff still has a weak heart as the result of an intentional inoculation with recurrent fever, and some of his collaborators have inoculated themselves with the most loathsome of diseases for the purpose of testing a remedy for it. Brown-Séquard, of the Collège de France, tried, at the age of seventy-two, to rejuvenate himself by injections of animal secretions, but his hopes proved unfounded.

But the means advocated by Metchnikoff for the prevention of senescence, even though it may never fulfill his expectations, has at least the merit of being harmless, for it is merely the systematic employment of a food which has been in use by a large part of the human race from the earliest times. The object being to colonize the lactic bacilli in the lower part of the digestive tract, the best way of attaining this has yet to be worked out. The generous drinking of buttermilk or curdled milk, though this may be nutritious or otherwise beneficial, does not necessarily accomplish the object, for the bacilli may have been mostly killed off by the acidity or may be destroyed in the stomach. Taking a dose of the bacilli in a dried form, as a tablet or powder, may fail to serve the purpose, because they are in an inactive state and may not be able to secure a foothold for lack of suitable food, such as milk or fruit sugar. So Metchnikoff has adopted the plan of taking pure cultures of the Bulgarian and paralactic bacilli in pasteurized milk or sweetened bouillon and also in the jam and in a kind of candy prepared from cooked dates soaked in the pure cultures. He abstains from all alcoholic beverages and uses only cooked food and boiled water. His daily diet in addition to this consists of three to five ounces of meat, grains, legumes, and stewed fruit.[1]

[1] See "Les Microbes lactiques et leur utilité pour la santé" in *La Revue*, 1901, p. 145. A full discussion of the subject of fermented milks with methods for their preparation in the household may be found in a volume by L. M. Douglas, recently published under the sensational title of "The Bacillus of Long Life" (Putnams).

This goes counter to the raw food advocates, but here Metchnikoff has the best of the argument. He also questions the advisability of excessive chewing as advocated by Mr. Fletcher, and cites cases where the health has been injured by the practice and the resulting disease cured by more rapid eating.[1]

As soon as Doctor Metchnikoff first made known his theory, the public, always on the lookout for a new "Elixir of Life", demanded fermented milk and the supply was immediately forthcoming, not always of a satisfactory character. Many of the cultures sold in powder or tabloids for the purpose or dispensed in drink at the soda fountains are inactive and useless, or contain other and sometimes undesirable forms of bacteria. I have found it easy enough to prepare the fermented milk in the household, where the proper cultures are to be had. All that is necessary is to sterilize the milk by heating it to the boiling point or near it and keeping it there for ten minutes; then cool quickly to 100° Fahr. and add the ferment in tabloids or powder or some of the former batch, and keep covered at this temperature for twelve hours. A vacuum bottle or fireless cooker is convenient for keeping the tempera-

[1] "The Prolongation of Life", p. 159.

[174]

ture even. The fermented milk properly prepared is somewhat thickened, slightly acid, and palatable even to those who do not like ordinary buttermilk.

Metchnikoff's views as to the value of lactic acid have met with not only the legitimate skepticism and criticism of the medical profession, but also with the usual ridicule from the press. "Who would want to live one hundred and fifty years if he had to drink sour milk three times a day ?" is asked, and he is alluded to as "the modern Ponce de Leon searching for the Fountain of Immortal Youth and finding it in the Milky Whey." Of course Metchnikoff should not be held responsible for the exaggerated expectations founded upon his theories or for the fakes foisted upon the public in his name. He is indeed an original thinker and a bold experimenter, but he is not a sensationalist or a seeker for popular applause. He has never said that he expected to live one hundred and fifty years or that any one else could by following his regimen. But he does regard that period as more nearly the normal length of human life than the commonly accepted limit of sixty-five or seventy, and as possibly attainable through the advance of medical science. Though he comes of a short-lived family and all his brothers died at an age much younger than he has now attained, his health is unusually good for a man of seventy, and he is as hard-working and enterprising as ever. It is not the mere prolongation of life for which he is working, but the prolongation of the period of serviceable and enjoyable life. If he had remained in the University of Odessa, he would have been retired from his professorship on the ground of old age in 1900, the year before he published his second and greatest work, that on " Immunity in Infectious Diseases."

The title which was given to his most popular book in its English version, "The Prolongation of Life", was not of his choosing and misrepresents his aim. He regards this volume as well as its predecessor, "The Nature of Man", as "Studies in Optimistic Philosophy." They are written to show that science is not merely of use in facilitating and ameliorating the lot of human beings, but is also adequate as a guide to conduct and capable of providing it with ideals of future aspiration. In an age when, as it appears to him, religion has lost its power, and thinking men no longer have faith in immortality, he sees them turning to mysticism on the one hand and to pessimism on the other, and his purpose is to find a way out that does not involve either. As an exposition of the Religio Medici of the twentieth

century, his work has great significance, and even
those who look with confidence to a future life to
rectify the disharmonies of this one may read with
interest the opinions of one who does not hold their
faith upon what may be accomplished toward per-
fecting the conditions of existence and may sympa-
thize with and second his efforts at such amelioration.

Essentially his aim seems to me to be the same
as that of Epicurus: to relieve mankind of its two
great evils, pain and fear, the fear of the gods and
the fear of death, the first to be dissipated by showing it to be imaginary and the second by welcoming
death at the proper time. Like Epicurus, too, but
unlike most Epicureans, Metchnikoff preaches plain
living and the avoidance of luxury and dissipation
of all kinds. "It would be true progress", he says,
"to abandon modern cuisine and go back to the
simpler dishes of our ancestors", and he objects
on hygienic grounds to modern dress, dwellings,
and social customs.

A society called "The Optimists" has been formed
in Paris to increase the sum and intensity of human
happiness and to extend the limit of active and
enjoyable life. The founder is Doctor E. Dagin-
court and the secretary is Mme. Languet de Bellevue,
who has given fifty thousand dollars to the move-

ment. Besides Professor Metchnikoff, the club includes Jean Finot, whose "Science of Happiness" and "Philosophy of Longevity" present similar ideals to Metchnikoff's "Optimistic Studies"; Camille Flammarion, the distinguished astronomer and author; Professor Charles Richet, who received the Nobel prize for medical discoveries in 1913; Eugene Brieux, author of "Damaged Goods" and other reform dramas; and Edmond Perrier, head of the Museum of Natural History.

Optimism Metchnikoff regards as the natural philosophy of old age when a proper appreciation of the value of life is attained and youthful pessimism outgrown.

In the normal course of life, however, the young do not show an instinctive clinging to life in any marked degree. They often risk their lives for trifling reasons and commit all sorts of indiscretions hurtful to life or health without a thought of the consequences. They may be inspired by the highest motives, but they are equally ready to fritter strength away in the gratification of the lowest appetites. Youth is the age of disinterested sacrifice, but also of indulgence in all kinds of excesses, alcoholic, sexual, and others. Youths seem to think that they will always attach the same value to life, and that between death at thirty years of age and death at sixty there is a difference only of time. As their love of life is indifferently developed, young people are often extremely exacting, the pleasure they

enjoy being but moderate, whilst the suffering pro-
voked in them by the slightest annoyance is intense.
They consequently become epicureans in the lowest
sense of the word, or else abandon themselves to
exaggerated pessimism. — "The Nature of Man",
p. 116.

Pessimism was the militant philosophy of the
nineteenth century, and its effects are increasingly
felt in the present world-wide tendency to suicide,
individual suicide due to the failure of the instinct
to live, and race suicide due to the failure to propagate. But even pessimism, harmful as it is upon
humanity, may, according to Metchnikoff, have its
uses :

It is pessimism which has been the first to draw up
a true indictment of human nature, and if pain is to
be regarded as useful in its quality of danger signal
we should equally recognize that the pessimistic
view of the universe is a step onward in the evolution
of humanity. Without pessimism we might easily
sink into a kind of contented fatalism, and end in
quietism, in the manner of many religions. —
"Nature of Man", p. 194.

The difference between the philosophic pessimist
and the scientific optimist may be illustrated by
two incidents. In 1831 Schopenhauer, in spite of
his theory that life was evil and worse than nothing,
fled from Berlin to Frankfort at the first outbreak
of the cholera. But we recall that Metchnikoff,

professed optimist and lover of life, went in 1911 to Manchuria into the center of the bubonic plague in its most virulent form in order to learn how to relieve human suffering. The difference is one between whiners and helpers.

Schopenhauer wrote that "an alteration of the atmosphere so slight that it cannot be detected by chemistry brings about cholera or yellow fever or black death." Metchnikoff's dry comment on this is: "Humanity will be fortunate if the pessimistic philosophers prove as wrong about their other grievances as they have proved about disease and medicine." And he adds that if Koch had discovered his vibrio in 1831, philosophy would have taken a different course, for Schopenhauer need not have been frightened away from Berlin, and Hegel, who died of the cholera, might have gone on with the development of his idealism.

Another paradox appears in the fact that Metchnikoff, who makes little account of altruism in his system of morality, has devoted his life to arduous and dangerous researches for the benefit of others, and, without hope of reward in another life in either the Buddhist or Christian sense, has labored assiduously to lay the foundations of a science by which posterity can profit. He regards altruism not as a permanent and indispensable virtue, but as something to be gradually got rid of, at least in its extreme forms of heroism and self-sacrifice. As this is one of the most striking and, it seems to me, most original points in his philosophy, a passage must be quoted :

As it is highly probable that with the advance of civilization the greatest evils of humanity will become lessened, and may even disappear, the sacrifices to be made will also become less. Now that there is a serum which protects against plague, there is no room for the heroism of the doctors who used to incur the greatest danger in fighting epidemics. Until lately doctors used to risk their life in treating the throats of diphtheritic patients. A young doctor who was a friend of mine, of high ability and promise, died from diphtheria contracted under these conditions. He met his death, in isolation from his friends in case of affecting them, with the utmost heroism. Now that the antidiphtheritic serum has been discovered, such heroism would be unnecessary. The advance of science has removed the occasion of such sacrifices.

It is now very long since there has been opportunity for the heroism which steeled the hand of Abraham to sacrifice his only son to his religion. Human sacrifice, based on the highest morality, has become more and more rare, and will finally disappear. Rational morality, although it may admire such conduct, has no use for it. So also it may foresee a time when men will be so highly developed that instead of being delighted to take advantage of the sympathy of their fellows, they will refuse it absolutely. Neither the Kantian idea of virtue, doing good as a pure duty, nor that of Herbert Spencer, according to which men have an instinctive need to help their fellows, will be realized in the future. The ideal will rather be that of men who will be self-sufficient and who will no longer permit others to do them good. — "Prolongation of Life", p. 323.

As he objects to conditions that demand sympathy and self-sacrifice from one person for another, so also he opposes any state of society that involves the sacrifice or subordination of the individual for the benefit of the community as a whole.

It is most probable that no shade of socialism will be able to solve the problem of social life with a sufficient respect for the maintenance of individual liberty. None the less the progress of human knowledge will inevitably bring about a great leveling of human fortunes. Intellectual culture will lead men to give up many things that are superfluous or even harmful, and that are still thought indispensable by most people. The conceptions that the greatest good fortune consists in the complete evolution of the normal cycle of human life and that this goal can be reached most easily by plain and sober habits will convince men of the folly of much of the luxury that now shortens human existence. Whilst the rich will choose a simpler mode of life and the poor will be able to live better, none the less, private property, acquired or inherited, may be maintained. Evolution must be gradual, and much effort and new knowledge is required. Sociology, a new-born science, must learn of biology, her older sister. Biology teaches us that in proportion that the organization becomes more complex, the consciousness of individuality develops, until a point is reached at which individuality cannot be sacrificed to the community. Amongst low creatures such as Myxomycetes and Siphonophora, the individuals disappear wholly or almost wholly in the community; but the sacrifice is small, as in these creatures the consciousness of individuality has not appeared. Social insects are in a stage intermediate between that of the lower animals and man. It is only in man that the individual has definitely acquired consciousness, and for that reason a satisfactory social organization cannot sacrifice it on pretext of the common good. To this conclusion the study of the social evolution of living beings leads me. It is plain that the study of human individuality is a necessary step in the organization of the social life of human beings. — "Prolongation of Life", p. 231.

One might think in reading "The Nature of Man" that Metchnikoff was laying the foundations of a pessimistic instead of an optimistic system of philosophy. He begins, as Schopenhauer or Von Hartmann might have done, by showing how ill adapted to his environment is that simian abortion we call man. Among the examples of marvelously perfect adaptation of structure or instinct in nature are cited Darwin's orchids and Fabre's wasps. M. Fabre seems to be indispensable to French philosophers. We have seen that Maeterlinck and Bergson get some of their finest illustrations from this "Homer of the Insects." But man is not so favored of nature as the orchids or wasps :

There can be no doubt but that the human constitution, although in many ways perfect and sublime, exhibits numerous and serious disharmonies which are the source of all our troubles. Not being so well adapted to the conditions of life as orchids are, for example, in the matter of their fertilization by the mediation of insects, or the burrowing wasps for the protection of their young, humanity resembles rather those insects the instinct of which guides them toward the flame which burns their wings.

In the first half of the nineteenth century there were published at the cost of five thousand dollars apiece eight volumes known as the Bridgewater Treatises on "The Power, Wisdom and Goodness of God as Manifested in the Creation," using as illustrations the structure of the hand, the instincts of animals, the chemistry of digestion, and other unworked sources of natural theology. The science was not bad for its time, nor was the argument altogether fallacious. But the authors overlooked one thing, namely, that Bridgewater is a game two can play at, and that it would be equally possible to fill eight other volumes by picking out a different set of facts, almost equally imposing, to prove something very different, either that there is no God or that there is a devil, either atheism or Manicheism. Metchnikoff's "Nature of Man" supplies much of the material that a devil's advocate might then have used in his Anti-Bridgewater Treatises.

But Metchnikoff, writing in the twentieth century, makes quite another use of it. He has doubtless never read the Bridgewater Treatises, nor have many of us. There is no reason to now. They have become waste paper, not because they were false, but because the whole mass of the argument against them has vanished, the half recognized and subconscious argument against theism derivable from the undeniable existence of disharmonies and imperfections in the universe. This battlefield is deserted; though the same struggle continues, it is on higher ground. This change has been wrought by the introduction of the idea of evolution. We now realize we do not live in a static universe. The theism which is founded on evolution may serenely acknowledge the discords and failures which would be fatal to the theism of the Bridgewater era. And Metchnikoff, as an atheist, is equally untroubled by the existence of misleading instincts and useless, disease-producing organs, for interpreting them in the light of evolution he escapes the

[185]

slough of nineteenth century pessimism and arrives triumphantly at the goal of optimism.

At least he says he does. I cannot see that his argument leads to optimism in the strict sense of the word, although it certainly leads him to a very sane and hopeful meliorism. The weakest point in his doctrine of orthobiosis seems to me his theory of euthanasia, that at the end of the "normal cycle" of life — whatever that may be — the desire for life is replaced by an instinct for death. The evidence he adduces in support of this is very scanty and questionable. It is curious to note that it was the experiences of Metchnikoff's brother which supplied Tolstoy with the material for the most harrowing picture of the fear of death in all literature, "The Death of Ivan Ilyitch."

In "The Prolongation of Life" Metchnikoff devotes much space to an analysis of the first and second parts of "Faust" and the life of Goethe, whom he manifestly regards as an excellent example of a complete and well-ordered life. The reader will observe that while he condemns Goethe's drinking habits because they undermined his constitution, he has, from the standpoint of a naturalist, no word of blame for his promiscuous love affairs, since these contributed to the development of his genius. This is, to say the least, a very one-sided view to take of it.

But this volume is concerned with the exposition rather than the criticism of the authors discussed, so I will conclude the chapter with a quotation which sums up his philosophy and sets forth his ideals:

In progress toward the goal, nature will have to be consulted continuously. Already, in the case of the ephemerids, nature has produced a complete cycle of normal life ending in natural death. In the problem of his own fate, man must not be content with the gifts of nature; he must direct them by his own efforts. Just as he has been able to modify the nature of animals and plants, man must attempt to modify his own constitution, so as to readjust its disharmonies.

Breeders form a conception of the ideal result when they are about to attempt the production of some new variety which shall be pleasing æsthetically and of service to man. Next, they study the existing individual variations in animals and plants on which they wish to work, and from which they will select with minutest care. The ideal result must have some relation to the constitution of the organism selected. To modify the human constitution, it will be necessary, first, to frame the ideal, and thereafter to set to work with all the resources of science.

If there can be formed an ideal able to unite men in a kind of religion of the future, this ideal must be founded on scientific principles. And if it be true, as has been asserted so often, that man can live by faith alone, the faith must be in the power of science. — "The Nature of Man", p. 302.

MAJOR PROPHETS OF TO-DAY

How to Read Metchnikoff

The philosophy of Metchnikoff is given in two volumes published in this country by Putnams, "The Nature of Man" and "The Prolongation of Life." The second and later volume will perhaps better serve the purpose of the general reader, but either will give the main outlines of his theories. Both volumes are written for the medical student rather than the public, and discuss some unpleasant subjects, but not in any objectionable manner. The English translation, at least in the first editions, is clumsy and careless. These works in the original are entitled "Essais sur la nature humaine", Paris, 1903, and "Essais optimistes", Paris, 1907. The German version, "Studien über die Natur des Menschen", Leipsic, 1904, is prefaced by Ostwald. "The New Hygiene", Three Lectures on the Prevention of Infectious Diseases, prefaced by Lankester, is published by W. T. Keever & Co., Chicago.

Articles by Metchnikoff easily accessible are: "Studies in Natural Death", in *Harper's Magazine*, Vol. CXIV, p. 272; "The Utility of Lactic Microbes", in *Century*, Vol. LXXIX, p. 53; "Old Age", in Smithsonian Report, 1904.

A criticism of Metchnikoff's individualism from a socialistic point of view is "The Optimism of Metchnikoff", by F. Carrel, in *Fortnightly Review*, Vol. LXXXIX, p. 51. A criticism to which Metchnikoff has made a reply in his second volume is "Morale et Biologie", by D. Parodi, in *Revue philosophique*, Vol. LVIII, p. 113. "Metchnikoff, philosophe" (Bibliothèque des Entretiens Idéalistes, Paris, 1911) is a pamphlet by a young Catholic, Fernand Divoire, in a style of frantic denunciation.

ÉLIE METCHNIKOFF

An interesting character sketch by A. McFarlane is to be found in *McClure's Magazine*, Vol. XXV, p. 541. Two interviews with Metchnikoff by Herman Bernstein are contained in *With Master Minds* (Universal Series Publishing Company New York). Sir Ray Lankester in his "Science from an Easy Chair" has a chapter on "Metchnikoff and Tolstoy."

Good articles on the theory of immunity as developed by Metchnikoff and others are: "The War Against Disease", in *Edinburgh Review*, October, 1910; "Paul Ehrlich: The Man and His Work", by Marguerite Marks, in *McClure's Magazine*, 1911, p. 184; "Natural Resistance to Disease", by Dr. Simon Flexner, of the Rockefeller Institute, in *Popular Science Monthly*, July, 1909, and in Smithsonian Report, 1909; "The Struggle for Immunity", by H. S. Williams, in *Harper's Magazine*, December, 1911. Circular No. 171 of the Bureau of American Industry of the United States Department of Agriculture gives a description of *Fermented Milks* by F. A. Rogers.

CHAPTER V

WILHELM OSTWALD

MAETERLINCK expresses his idea of happiness through the symbol of the Blue Bird. Ostwald expresses his by

$$G = E^2 - W^2$$

Poets and scientists both are necessarily symbolists. The apparent conflict between them is chiefly a difference of taste as to the choice of symbols, for both stand together in opposition to the great mass of near-sighted humanity, those who live only in the concrete, too absorbed in the consideration of particulars to discover for themselves the One in the Many. The most conspicuous difference between the symbolism of poetry and that of science is that the former is old and the latter new. The poet prefers to go to antiquity for symbols, bringing down from the attic to the living-room some metaphorical heirloom, enriched by the associations of generations and carrying with it a penumbra of indefinable suggestions, which makes it appear to mean more than it does. So Maeterlinck chooses for his fairy play "The Blue Bird", which had lived in folk lore for countless ages. But the scientist prefers to invent a new symbol for the occasion in order to get something that shall convey neither more nor less meaning than what he himself puts into it at the time. Poets and artists of all sorts get credit for greater perspicacity and prophetic power than they deserve, by reason of later generations reading into their sayings much more meaning than was ever in the mind of the author. This unearned increment of reputation, compounded annually, is all that keeps some ancient authors alive nowadays. But the man of science disdains such support and is careful to define his terms so that posterity may give him no more credit than he thinks he has earned by his own exertions.

The scientific symbolism is not only more exact than the poetic, but it is also more practical. Doubtless "The Blue Bird" of Maurice Maeterlinck and "The Blue Flower" of Henry Van Dyke have contributed to happiness as well as stood for it, but they are not of much service in showing which of two courses in any dilemma will lead to it. The unpoetical reader might suppose that to be blue was to be happy. Ostwald, however, insists that his formula is not a mere mathematical jest, but applicable to practical affairs, and like a true physician he has tried it on himself and knows that it works. He tells us that he solved one of the most difficult problems of his life by its aid, as, for example, when at the age of fifty-three the question arose whether he should remain professor of chemistry in Leipzig University or retire to his country place at Gross-Bothen to take up the new profession of "practical idealist."

An interpretation of Ostwald's formula for happiness,

$$G = E^2 - W^2$$

will enable the reader to try it for himself. G stands for happiness (*Glück*). This, according to the theory of energetics, is dependent upon the amount of energy expended, might in fact be measured by the amount of carbon dioxid produced by conscious activity if we could separate this from the unconscious physiological processes of the body. Part of this Energy is expended in agreeable ways; let that be represented by E. But there is always another part of conscious activity which is unpleasant, such as painful feelings, disagreeable thoughts, unwilling duties; that may be represented by W (*widerwillig*).

WILHELM OSTWALD

The second term $(E^2 - W^2)$ of the equation may be resolved into the two factors $E + W$ and $E - W$, and increase of either will tend to increase the amount of happiness. The way of the strenuous life is to increase the first $(E + W)$, the total expenditure of energy; that is, to exert one's self to the utmost in desired directions, even though opposition and anxieties increase also; to bring up the health to its highest point that the supply of chemical energy may not fail; to cut down as much as possible on sleep, for that is the time when both E and W sink to zero. This is what Ostwald calls Hero-happiness (*Heldenglück*).

But men of more timid temperament prefer to devote their attention to the other factor $(E - W)$, because herein lies the danger, not merely of no happiness (when $G = O$), but of unhappiness, for G becomes a minus quantity when W is greater than E. They strive rather to reduce W, the unpleasant part of life, than to increase E, the pleasant. To avoid risks, to curb ambition, to limit desires, to curtail expenditure, to seek contentment rather than delight — this is the way of the simple life and leads to Hut-happiness (*Hüttenglück*). This may indeed attain the same result, give an equal value for G, but the happiness so reached is very

[193]

different in kind, though equivalent in degree, to that for which strive men of the type of Napoleon, Edison, and Roosevelt. The search for happiness by limitation instead of expansion leads at its extreme to stoicism, to asceticism, to nirvana, to the state of mind of Diogenes, who threw away his sole utensil, the cup, when he saw a man drink out of his hand.

Many moralists before Ostwald have attempted to put this idea into semi-mathematical form, generally with the object of advising the seeker after happiness to take the lower and smoother road. Carlyle says in " Sartor Resartus":

"The Fraction of Life can be increased in value, not so much by increasing your Numerator as by lessening your Denominator. Nay, unless my Algebra deceive me, Unity itself divided by Zero will give Infinity. Make thy claim of wages a zero, then; thou hast the world at thy feet. Well did the Wisest of our time write 'It is only with Renunciation that Life, properly speaking, can be said to begin.'"

James, in his "Principles of Psychology", expresses it as follows:

$$\text{Self-esteem} = \frac{\text{Success.}}{\text{Pretensions.}}$$

That is, our self-esteem is determined by the ratio

of our actualities to our supposed potentialities. And he suggests that some Bostonians "would be happier men and women to-day if they could once for all abandon the notion of keeping up a Musical Self and without shame let people hear them call a symphony a nuisance."

William Winter puts the thought in rhyme:

"I have set my heart on nothing, you see
And so the world goes well with me."

One is irresistibly impelled to quote Johnson's remark:

"Sir, that all who are happy, are equally happy, is not true. A peasant and a philosopher may be equally *satisfied*, but not equally *happy*. Happiness consists in the multiplicity of agreeable consciousness. A peasant has not capacity for having equal happiness with a philosopher."

Boswell tags this in his usual style with the observation that this very question was "very happily illustrated" by the Reverend Mr. Robert Brown at Utrecht, who said that "a small drinking glass and a very large one may be equally full, but the large one holds more than the small."

Ostwald applies his formula to James's "Varieties of Religious Experience", and shows that the convert leaves the mourner's bench at the moment when the factor $(E - W)$ changes its sign from minus to plus. (Here W apparently stands for the devil.) The equation also serves him as an argument against the use of alcohol and other narcotics, which, though they temporarily reduce W by sinking all unpleasantnesses below the threshold of consciousness, are likely to make happiness a minus quantity. Wealth, being the most compact and convenient form of energy, may serve to increase E or diminish W, but not in proportion to its amount. Dramatic criticism may even be made mathematical. Jaques has a large W; Rosalind has a large E; put them together and you have "As You Like It."

But I should not devote so much space to what is merely an extreme and, some would say, an extravagant application of Ostwald's philosophy.[1] It is, however, a characteristic example of his mode of thought and may serve as well as any other to introduce the reader to his fundamental theory of energetics, which formed the leading principle of his chemical work, and which he has now carried over into the fields of philosophy and sociology.

It is not necessary to explain the modern conception of energy, for we all learned about it in our

[1] The reader who is interested and reads German will find a full discussion of the formula and its significance in *Die Forderung des Tages*.

school days, and here we need only have in mind its two fundamental laws. The first is the law of the conservation of energy, discovered by Mayer, which states that the amount of energy remains unchanged whatever its transformations. To take a familiar example, when we buy coal, we are really buying chemical energy, not carbon. When we burn it, we let the carbon go off up the chimney, but the heat energy we keep as completely as possible, and by means of a boiler transform it into the expansive energy of steam, which is converted into the motion energy of piston rod and wheel, and when connected with a dynamo may become electrical energy. The electrical energy we can conduct by a wire into our homes and there convert it into the light energy of an incandescent bulb, the heat energy of an electric griddle, or the motion energy of a fan or carpet sweeper. That is, whenever any kind of energy disappears, some other kind of energy crops up somewhere in exactly equivalent amount. In any experiment where they can be measured, the income and outgo of energy will be found to balance exactly, just like a bookkeeper's ledger.

But here is another thing to consider. The fact that a trial balance comes out even does not prove that the concern is not losing money, and we see the same thing in the energy business. In the series of transformations we have followed above, from the coal of the power house to the utensils of the household, there is leakage all along the line, a little lost in friction and radiated heat in each of the machines, and a big waste, some eighty-five per cent, in the steam engine. Ostwald uses the ingenious illustration of a traveler who goes through Europe changing his money at every frontier, and losing a little each time through the changer's discount. A good money changer is one who is satisfied with a moderate commission. A good machine is one that gives back to us almost as much as we give it. But there is none perfect, no, not one.

This is the second fundamental law of thermodynamics,[1] the law of the degradation of energy. For energy has a sort of gravitation of its own. It always wants to run down hill. Heat seeks its level as well as water. If we lay a hot plate, say, a temperature of 100°, on or under a plate at zero, the heat will spread to the cold plate until both are at 50°, disregarding radiation losses. And when they have come to the same temperature, it is im-

[1] My unconventional definitions of the second law would be repudiated by any self-respecting physicist. The reader is therefore warned that the proper way to say it is, "the entropy of the universe tends to a maximum." (Clausius.)

[198]

possible to get out of them any further heat movement. "You cannot run the mill with the water
that's gone by." You have to have a fall of temperature to run any kind of heat engine. Every
machine, every chemical and physical process, every
living being, is leaking energy all the time, that is,
transforming it into unavailable forms. That is
the way we get our living. The sun is dissipating
its heat energy throughout space at a great rate.
Our allies, the plants, manage to catch a tiny bit
of it and store it in starch and oil, but we eat these
and send the energy on its way as heat again. The
whole universe, regarded as a big machine, is running
down like a clock and, it seems, must ultimately
come to a stop, unless, indeed, there is a self-wind-
ing attachment hidden away in it somewhere, or
somebody outside of it all to wind it up occasionally.

This, however, is one of those questions which
Ostwald calls "pseudo-problems" and from which
he would free us by applying the energetic philosophy. His test is the following: "Suppose the
problem solved and assume any one of all possible
answers to be correct, we can then investigate what
effect this would have on our conduct. If it pro-
duces no effect, the problem is thereby indicated to

be a pseudo-problem." He takes for example the following :

> Did the world have a beginning in time or has it existed from all eternity ? By the way of experiment we will assume that it has existed since eternity, and will ask what would change in our conduct by this knowledge ? I find, at least for myself, that nothing would change by this knowledge, and just as little if we assume that there was a beginning in time. Hence I must say that even if I positively learn in some way which of the two possibilities is correct, it would be a matter of perfect indifference to me, and this being the case, we have here a pseudo-problem. The significance of this procedure is apparent from the answer to the question as to what we call "correct" or "true." The answer was that which enables us to make accurate predictions. Something that does not allow us to make any prediction whatever is essentially of no interest to us in any way, and there is no need of being concerned about it. — "The Modern Theory of Energetics" (*Monist*, 1907).

This, of course, is the pragmatic method, and Ostwald acknowledges the relationship by observing : " Energetics coincides with that movement which has originated on philosophical ground and which pursues very similar ends under the name of pragmatism or humanism." The pragmatic mode of thinking is practically universal among scientific men, but Ostwald is an extreme pragmatist. Prophecy is the sole aim of science, according to him, and he virtually denies the possibility of applying the terms truth and falsehood, in the strict sense, to the statements of history.[1]

To catch what we can of this stream of energy and to utilize it to the best advantage, is the aim of human endeavor, the measure of civilization. This is the function of the will in the individual and the duty of the leaders of men. Wealth in all ages consists essentially of the command of energy, whether counted by slave power, horse power, or kilowatt hours. In order to show how Ostwald's sociology grows out of his physics, let me quote the concluding paragraphs of his little book on "Natural Philosophy":

The objective characteristic of progress consists in improved methods for seizing and utilizing the raw energies of nature for human purposes. Thus it was a cultural act when a primitive man discovered that he could extend the radius of his muscle energy by taking a pole in his hand, and it was another cultural act when a primitive man discovered that by throwing a stone he could send his muscle energy a distance of many meters to the desired point. The effect of the knife, the spear, the arrow, and of all the other primitive implements can be called in each case a purposive transformation of energy. And at the other end of the scale of civilization the most abstract

[1] *Was ist Wahrheit?* (*Monistiche Sonntagspredigten, Nr. 5*).

scientific discovery, by reason of its generalization and simplification, signifies a corresponding economy of energy for all the coming generations that may have anything to do with the matter. Thus, in fact, the concept of progress as here defined embraces the entire sweep of human endeavor for perfection, or the entire field of culture, and at the same time it shows the great scientific value of the concept of energy.

If we consider further that, according to the second fundamental principle, the free energy accessible to us can only decrease, but not increase, while the number of men whose existence depends directly on the consumption of a due amount of free energy is constantly on the increase, then we at once see the objective necessity of the development of civilization in that sense. His foresight puts man in a position to act culturally. But if we examine our present social order from this point of view, we realize with horror how barbarous it still is. Not only do murder and war destroy cultural values without substituting others in their place, not only do the countless conflicts which take place between the different nations and political organizations act anticulturally, but so do also the conflicts between the various social classes of one nation, for they destroy quantities of free energy which are thus withdrawn from the total of real cultural values. At present mankind is in a state of development in which progress depends much less upon the leadership of a few distinguished individuals than upon the collective labor of all workers. Proof of this is that it is coming to be more and more the fact that great scientific discoveries are made simultaneously by a number of independent investigators — an indication that society

creates in several places the individual conditions
requisite for such discoveries. Thus we are living at
a time when men are gradually approximating one
another very closely in their natures, and when the
social organization therefore demands and strives
for as thorough an equalization as possible in the
conditions of existence of all men.

From the same fundamental conception Ostwald
derives his system of ethics, which he sums up in
"the energetic imperative": [1] *So act that the crude
energy is transformed into the higher with the least
possible loss.* This forms the text of several of his
lay sermons such as the one on "Efficiency." [2]
Efficiency, that is, the ratio of work to means, of
accomplishment to opportunity, can be made the
measure of a man as well as of a machine, since
Ostwald includes all thoughts and feelings as forms
of energy. This scientific conception and ideal
of efficiency, developed in the laboratory, was first
introduced into the shop, thence it has crept into
business management, and has even made its unwelcome appearance in university administration.
It cannot be much longer kept out from the capitol,
the church, and the home. It is, in fact, the contribution to our civilization by the fourth and newest

[1] *Der energetische Imperativ, Ann. d. Nat. Phil.*, Vol. X.
[2] Printed in *The Independent*, October 19, 1911.

of the learned professions, that of the engineer. He it is who has started us all wondering how much of what we daily do pays us in any coin, has made us anxious to see some relation between effort and result, has rendered us impatient of unnecessary delay, friction, lost motion, wasted work, unutilized material, and retarded rewards.

To distinguish low and high forms of energy, says Ostwald, we should consider their relative importance for human purposes. Thus bread must be regarded as containing a higher form of chemical energy than wood, although they are very similar in chemical composition and produce about the same number of calories of heat on consumption.

Kant's categorical imperative, "So act that your conduct may be taken as a universal law", is, in Ostwald's opinion, neither so comprehensive nor so definite as his energetic imperative, which includes ethical conduct, but is not confined to it. We call one automobile "good" and another "bad" if the former will carry us twice as far as the latter on the same amount of gasoline consumed. A "good" friend is one who helps us in our endeavors through judicious advice and without annoyance, while a "poor" friend only multiplies our difficulties; here again goodness and badness are determined by the ratio of the total energy employed and the results obtained. It is this second principle of thermodynamics, the law of the degradation and dissipation of energy, that prevents us from undoing the past, that gives significance to such phrases as "time flies" and "the world moves." The cosmic process is not a reversible reaction. Nietzsche's nightmare of the eternal recurrence, which drove him insane, would have been dispelled by a knowledge of elementary physics.

The second law is therefore of greater importance to philosophy and sociology than the first, the law of the conservation and transmutation of energy. Ostwald's recognition of its significance gives to his philosophy a character decidedly different from the view dominant in the last century, the mechanistic theory of the universe. It is a curious thing that Haeckel, the biologist, has, by basing his philosophy on the first law, been led to extreme mechanistic views, while Ostwald, the physical chemist, by placing greater emphasis upon the second law, comes to conclusions much better suited to the explanation of vital phenomena.

According to the old mechanistic theory, the world could be reduced to two elements, matter and motion. Everything was held to consist in reality of atoms, in those days generally assumed to be indivisible and eternal. Each atom was at a given instant moving in a certain direction at a certain speed. It followed from this, as was suggested in the *Philosophical Magazine* many years ago, that if each atom should be suddenly stopped and sent going back on its track with the same speed, all events would be reversed and history be repeated backward. If we were watching Waterloo, for example,[1] we should see the dead men rise up one by one, pick up their guns, point them at their enemies, receive into the gunbarrels the gases produced by the explosion of powder, and walk off backward. Napoleon starting as a prisoner on St. Helena would end as Emperor of the French.

We have all of us had this idea pictorially presented to us in moving picture shows when the film is run through the lantern backward and we see apples leaping from the ground and attaching themselves to the limbs of the tree, and swimmers diving up out of the water and lighting on the springboard. In fact, the reversed film of the cinematograph may be regarded as the *reductio ad absurdum* of the mechanistic hypothesis. We might expect that a piece of music would sound just as

[1] See Flammarion's scientific fantasy, *Lumen*.

well if we put the perforated paper roll into the
player piano wrong end first — but somehow it
doesn't. We all feel instinctively that there is
something ridiculous and impossible about this idea
of reversibility when applied to human beings.
Even the chemist and the physicist can effect this
reversibility only to a limited extent and in special
cases, as, for example, when energy is supplied from
some external source. A sled can indeed be made
to go up hill as well as down, but it is hard work to
make it. Wood will burn easily, but no chemist
is yet able to get the wood back out of the gases
of combustion. The second energy law was taught
to us in our infancy by the parable of Humpty-
Dumpty.

Bergson bases his theory of the comic [1] upon the
idea that the absurdest of all things is to regard a
human being as a machine. That the world is, like
man, not rightly to be regarded as a machine is the
fundamental theme of Bergson's "Creative Evolution", so there is a striking similarity in point of
view between Ostwald and Bergson, notwithstanding their diversity of temperament and style. It
may be recalled that Bergson also entered into the

[1] Laughter. An Essay on the Meaning of the Comic. By Henri
Bergson. The Macmillan Company.

realm of metaphysics through the door of mathematical physics.

As early as 1895 Ostwald announced "the overthrow of scientific materialism"; [1] a startling declaration coming from one of the greatest of chemists at a time when chemistry was almost exclusively absorbed in the transformations of matter and only beginning to recognize the importance of the concomitant transformations of energy. When the chemist had put upon the blackboard the equation of a reaction or the structural formula of a compound, he was apt to think that he had told "the truth, the whole truth and nothing but the truth" about it. Against all such crude conceptions Ostwald protested vigorously, preaching a new iconoclasm in the words of the old: "Thou shalt not make unto thee any image or any likeness of anything that is in the heaven above, or that is in the earth beneath, or that is in the water under the earth; thou shalt not bow down thyself to them, nor serve them." He demanded "a science free from hypotheses"; formulas that should merely state what is known to take place, in the place of mechanical models and misleading visualizations. "Matter", said this

[1] Die Ueberwindung des wissenschaftlichen Materialismus. Lübeck address before the German Association of Naturalists and Physicians.

professor of the most materialistic of the sciences, "is merely a form of thought", which is the same conclusion that Kant had come to a hundred years before in regard to time and space. But whereas Kant had said: "Give me matter and I will build a world out of it", Ostwald would say: "Away with matter, I will build a world without it."

"The Actual, that is, what acts upon us, is energy alone", but in so speaking Ostwald must not be understood, as he often is, to imply that energy is the sole substance of which the world is composed. Mass is merely one of the two factors which make up the product known as energy. What the common man regards as the attributes of matter, its hardness, heaviness, color, etc., are simply the effects of various forms of energy on his sense organs.

Coal should be sold by calories, not tons. Even the courts, slowest of human institutions to take cognizance of new ideas, have come to the conclusion that energy is an entity, for now they will convict a man for stealing it from a third rail, though perhaps they regard the current as a stream of corpuscles. The unifying value of the energy conception appears when we consider the old riddle of the relation of the mind and body. Between the brain, regarded merely as a collocation of moving molecules, and the mind, regarded merely as a succession of states of consciousness, there is no conceivable connection, and dualism is inevitable. But if we regard both as forms of energy, the difficulty disappears. The "preëstablished harmony" of Leibnitz then becomes the established unity of Ostwald. The idea of energy had its inception in human action, so it is not an alien form of thought. It was borrowed originally from psychology by physics, and there is no impropriety in taking it back.

What we have been calling explanations in physics, and even in psychology, have been for the most part merely mechanical analogies. We have felt that a phenomenon was "explained" when we could make a working model that we could see and handle. A few years ago physicists were explaining electricity by cumbrous mechanisms of cogwheels and water pipes. In recent textbooks this is reversed, and mechanical phenomena are explained by the use of conceptions developed in the study of electricity, such as "potential", "field", and "capacity."

The establishment in 1901 of the *Annalen der Naturphilosophie*, by Wilhelm Ostwald, marked the change in the attitude of prominent scientists toward the problems of speculative philosophy. The pendulum was on its swing back from the extreme and intolerant empiricism which has **been** the prevailing trait of scientific workers for so long.

In its revulsion from the imaginative metaphysics of the ancients and the formal logic of the school-men, modern science resolutely turned away from ambitious attempts to solve the riddle of the universe by brilliant guessing and began the patient accumulation and verification of facts and the deduction from them of their simplest and most certain inferences. This task came to be considered as the sole sphere of scientific thought; and there were men who were daring and foolish enough to teach that this was the only method for the advancement of human knowledge. Happily, however, for civilization, scientists did not confine themselves to the method prescribed for them by Bacon and other literary men, and of late years it has become generally recognized that the greatest achievements have been made in quite the opposite way — that is, by projecting the imagination into the unknown and then working up to it. Almost all the best scientific work has been done under the guidance of hypotheses; and purely accidental discoveries have been rare and usually insignificant. In fact, in many branches of science the word invention should be used rather than discovery. The new compound

[211]

or the new plant exists clearly in the mind's eye of the chemist or the horticulturist before he sets out to produce it.

It was not to be expected that men who had already accomplished more in science in a century than had been done in all preceding time would forever keep their trained imaginations from attacking the deepest problems of life and destiny; and it is no wonder that we find some of our greatest scientists turning their attention toward metaphysics and epistemology. The transfer of Professor Mach from the chair of physics to that of the theory of inductive sciences was symbolic of a mental change which was taking place in many minds.

The removal of the ban against speculative philosophy has obviously its dangers, but they are less than have been attached to this form of thought in the past. That mankind should again go back to the sports of its youth and blow soap bubbles merely to watch in them the iridescent but distorted views of the world would be a sad calamity; but it is not probable that the lesson of a century and a half of patient work will be wholly lost. The dreamer of the future will not dare to build an air castle without at least an option on the site. The danger is not from men of science like Ostwald,

Mach, and Poincaré, who are so well ballasted that they can carry more sail than ordinary men, but from those who are less qualified and less cautious. We have never, however, been free from the fancies of this latter class. Nature abhors a vacuum; and if any field of intellect is left empty by the wise but overwary, it will speedily be filled by those who have no fears where they tread. The recrudescence of antiquated superstitions and the rise of freak religions are the natural result of confining scientific thought and criticism to the material and practical. Even the plodding compilator of facts has his metaphysical theories, although he would indignantly deny that anything of the kind could be found about his person. Metaphysics may be ignored, but not dispensed with. In the so-called "common sense" point of view, speculative hypotheses are not excluded, but are unconsciously and uncritically accepted.

Science has evidently been looking on the ground only to be sure of her footing, and now is ready to assert her right to gaze even into the deepest darknesses. No Baconian creed will in the future limit the operations of the intellect. We have no right to call any problem insoluble merely because it has remained unsolved. It may be that as great triumphs will reward the scientific method here as in humbler lines.

In the revolution which has within the last twenty years transformed chemistry from an empirical science based upon material conceptions to a mathematical science based upon energetic conceptions, Ostwald has been a leader. Qualitative and quantitative analysis which had been hardly more systematic and rational than a kitchen recipe book became in his hands a new and delightful study in which even the beginner could use his mind as well as his fingers. Professors of chemistry who had got along happily all their lives with a knowledge of arithmetic as far as and including percentage suddenly found themselves in need of calculus and other things of that sort. Yale graduates who went to the Leipzig laboratory in the nineties to continue their chemistry were set to study the works of Willard Gibbs, whose name they may indeed have seen in the catalogue of their alma mater, but whose acquaintance they were not likely to have made. What was worse, they had to get up their Gibbs in German,[1] since the original papers in the "Transactions of the Connecticut Academy" were not avail-

[1] J. Willard Gibbs: "Thermodynamische Studien." Uebersetzt von W. Ostwald. Leipzig: W. Engelmann. 1892.

able, and even in English Gibbs is not light reading. It was Ostwald who first recognized Gibbs as "the greatest scientific genius that the United States has so far produced", and made his work known to Europe, where it has served as the guide and inspiration of some of the most fruitful investigations of the last two decades.

This is eminently characteristic of Ostwald. His own researches, great as they are, may without injustice be regarded as of less importance than the unique service he has rendered to his science by the discovery and prompt utilization of original theories and generalizations, whether found in the forgotten files of the journals and transactions, in the papers of his contemporaries or the work of his students. This was a task requiring both genius and generosity. What he did for Gibbs, the American, he did for van't Hoff, the Dutchman, and Arrhenius, the Swede, and many others, living and dead. He has always taken a keen interest in individuals. He is not content with the mere name of a great authority in a footnote. He wants to know what manner of man he was and in what words he first made public his discovery. This led him to cultivate the neglected field of chemical history and biography. Most chemists knew nothing at first hand of the work of the men they glibly referred to in their lectures, Avogadro, Bunsen, Dalton, Berzelius, etc. Nor could they have easily become acquainted with them if they had cared to, for the original papers were often inaccessible. So Ostwald started in 1889 his series of "The Classics of the Exact Sciences", reprinting important papers with notes.

In 1887, when few people knew that there was such a thing as physical chemistry, he founded a journal for it, the *Zeitschrift für physikalische Chemie*, now in its eighty-first volume, and not room enough yet in its two thousand three hundred pages a year to record the progress of the science. In 1902, when most scientists scoffed at the idea of philosophy, he started another venture equally bold, the *Annalen der Naturphilosophie*. During this period of sixteen years his literary output, not counting the two periodicals and the eighteen volumes of the "Classics of the Exact Sciences", already mentioned, included twenty-two books of 15,850 pages altogether; 120 papers making original contributions to chemical science comprising 1630 pages; addresses and dissertations amounting to 300 pages; and some 3880 abstracts and 920 book reviews in his journals. Every chemical library has upon its shelves (the plural is usually necessary) "the big Ostwald," the "Lehrbuch der allgemeinen Chemie", the size of a cyclopedia, with the dates of its volumes strung along through the eighties and nineties, though "the little Ostwald", the "Grundriss der allgemeinen Chemie", shows more wear on the binding. And all that, it must be remembered, represents only one side of the activity of this extraordinary man, for during the period of this enormous literary production he was professor of chemistry at the University of Leipzig and director of one of the busiest research laboratories in the world.

We find in our American universities nowadays many men who are so absorbed in their investigations that they refuse to consider either the philosophical or the practical aspects of their science, and they resent as an insult any demands made upon their time by the outside world. Ostwald has never been so busy as that. Notwithstanding the fact that he has carried on researches in pure science which have obtained for him the Nobel prize, he has not disdained to print letters to painters on the use of pigments and to lecture to housewives on the chemistry of cooking, as well as to bring his knowledge of science to bear upon the educational, social, and religious questions discussed in the periodicals of the day.

When we inquire why no American chemist has yet been honored by a Nobel medal, we are apt to be told that laboratory facilities in this country are too inadequate. Ostwald has never been hindered by this obstacle; not in Riga, where he was his own mechanic and glass blower, equipping the laboratory with home-made burettes, induction coils, and galvanometers; not in Leipzig, where he worked under conditions that have been described as follows : [1]

" The Leipzig laboratory, in which he worked until 1897, was situated in the Landwirtschaftliche Institut, an old pile originally devoted to agricultural chemistry, and in every way unfitted for the carrying on of those delicate experiments which brought Ostwald to the forefront of scientific workers. Research was carried on under countless difficulties; the light was bad, the rooms unventilated, the heating effected by means of stoves difficult to regulate and producing dust which caused much injury to the finer instruments; no precautions had been taken in laying the foundations to insure the deadening of vibrations; thus many experiments were ruined; the lack of space precluded the use of telescopes for reading scales, and altogether it would have been difficult to

[1] *Nature*, 64, 428 (1901).

construct a laboratory worse adapted for physico-
chemical investigations."

In one respect, it must be said, the current of
scientific thought has gone quite counter to Ostwald's
views. The atomic theory, which he was desirous
of doing away with, has become substantiated and
extended. The kinetic theory of gases has not been
displaced by his concept of "volume-energy", and
now the motion of the molecules has been made
visible by the ultra-microscope, and we hear talk
of the "atomic theory of electricity", the "corpus-
cular conception of light", and the "granular nature
of energy." Even time and space show a tendency
to disintegrate and become discrete. But the tide
may turn at any moment, and Ostwald's conceptions once more become fashionable in scientific
circles.

As I say, Ostwald does not appear to be a busy
man. Would a busy man take the heart out of a
fair summer day to devote himself to the entertainment of a wandering American journalist? If
I had not known that he was an editor of two periodicals and a leader in some of the most important
movements of the day, I might have supposed him
a mere gentleman of leisure, as he sat with me on
the porch of his country home, willing to talk freely

on any topic I suggested, willing even to listen when I wanted to talk, with never a longing look through his study door at the heavily laden desk and silent typewriter. A big man, as well as a great man, is Ostwald; genial in manner, direct of speech. His bushy blond beard has mostly lost the color it had when first I saw him in 1904 at the St. Louis Congress of Arts and Sciences, and his hair is quite white and now cut short, bristling an inch or two all over his head. He would be recognized as a German professor by his look and bearing, if he were seen anywhere on the globe, yet he could not be called a type specimen, for he is free from the vices to which the average German professor is most addicted, the love of beer, tobacco, and Latin. Also, he hates dueling, although recognizing that it is not so dangerous as American football.[1]

But unconventional as his views may appear, it must not be thought that Ostwald is a faddist. His is a reasoned radicalism, originating not in mere neophilism or iconoclasm, but in the application of scientific principles to the problems of daily life. What distinguishes Ostwald from most other philosophers is his willingness to put his principles to the test of experience by striving to live up to them.

[1] "Kultur und Duell" in "Die Forderung des Tages."

WILHELM OSTWALD

Our conversation was in English necessarily, for though I had taken my first German lessons from Ostwald over twenty years before — using his "Lehrbuch der allgemeinen Chemie" as a primer, instead of Grimm's "Märchen" — he had not been at hand to teach me to speak it. Ostwald, however, speaks English as readily as he does German — or French or Ido. His biographer relates that when he was learning English in the Riga *Gymnasium* he had great difficulty in pronouncing "the", until he discovered that he could get the sound by filling his mouth with *Zwieback;* on the same principle, I suppose, as Demosthenes used pebbles. Now, however, he manages his *th*'s perfectly, and I don't think he had *Zwieback* in his mouth when he talked with me.

His language was particularly fluent and forcible when he came to discuss the question of teaching languages. The chief point in his indictment of the German *Gymnasium*, or secondary school, is the excessive time and excessive honor given to linguistics. He regards the new scientific school (*Realschule*) as almost as bad as the classical *Gymnasium* in this respect, for modern languages are there taught in much the same way as the ancient. The absorption of the student's attention during

the impressionable years of his youth in the idio-
syncrasies of German grammar, or the monstrosities
of English spelling, does not cultivate, but actually
impairs, the power of logical and original thinking.
Ostwald ascribes Nietzsche's perverted ideas, his
misconception of the struggle for existence and his
hatred of the common people, to his training in
classical philology. He brings forward as a cause
of the failure of Austria-Hungary to produce its
proportional share of great men, the linguistic
struggle which absorbs the energy of its people.
The barrier of local language is one of the causes
of international friction and lost motion which
grieves the mind of a physicist. As a means of
overcoming this friction — a linguistic lubricating
oil, as it were — he favors the formation of an international auxiliary language, especially for scientific and commercial purposes.[1] I suppose one

[1] Ostwald devoted the $40,000 he got from the Nobel Fund to the
attempt to introduce a new language, Ido. Mistral devoted his to the
attempt to perpetuate an old language, Provençal. So we see that
dynamite money, like dynamite itself, exerts its force in opposite directions.

Ido is a simplified form of Esperanto, originating in the refusal of
Dr. Zamenhof to allow any reforms in the language he had invented.
It drops the accented letters and accusative form of Esperanto and
utilizes a larger proportion of romance roots common to all European
languages. The official organs are *Progreso* (Paris : 3 Rue le Gof) and

reason why he thinks it possible to construct an artificial world language is because he has seen it done. The rapid expansion of the science of organic chemistry within the present generation has necessitated the invention, as the need for them arose, of more new words than Shakespeare's vocabulary contained. Some of these are cumbrous, it is true, rather formulas than words, but remarkable for their succinct significance and are largely common to all languages. Ostwald has recently constructed a complete new nomenclature of chemistry in Ido and proposes soon to use it for all the abstracts in his *Zeitschrift für physikalische Chemie,* so that the student, after a few hours spent in learning Ido, will have free access to all the literature of this science. Professor Ostwald assured me that he had tried putting his philosophy into the new language and found it of great benefit in giving clarity and definiteness to his thought. The adoption of

---

The International Language (London: 32 Cleveland Square). Ostwald's new chemical nomenclature began in the May, 1910, number of *Progreso.* The volume by Ostwald, Jespersen, and three other professors entitled "International Language and Science" (London: Constable, 1910), contains an interesting test of the capabilities of the new language, the translation into Ido and back again into English by another person of a page of James's psychology with almost no loss in the process. A page of "Das Monistische Jahrhundert" appears each week in Ido.

an international language he regards as an important part of the peace movement in which he is now actively engaged. I asked him if he expected that arbitration treaties would put an end to war, and he explained that they would act like a block signal system on a railroad, not always preventing the disaster of war, but lessening the chances of it.

In order to give effect to practical measures for breaking down the barriers between nations, he has established "An International Institute for the Organization of Intellectual Labor" known as *Die Brücke*, "The Bridge", or, as he would prefer to put it in Ido, *La Ponto*. This aims to serve the purpose of a world clearing house of information and a channel of intercourse for all forms of culture. A plan for a uniform system of page sizes for books and periodicals, "the hypotenuse oblong", has been here brought forward and is discussed in *Printing Art*, April and May, 1911, July, 1912.

So Ostwald, having won the Nobel chemistry prize in 1909, is in a fair way to become in time eligible for the Nobel peace prize. It is in fact characteristic of the man that, having achieved success in one field of human endeavor, he should turn his attention to another. It is part of his theory of the art of life. I was curious to know why he

[224]

had left Leipzig and chemistry for Gross-Bothen and philosophy, had abandoned one of the greatest of universities and the most popular of the sciences for the Saxon village and a field of thought reputed as unproductive. He explained to me that in early years he had a leaning toward philosophy, but in those days the subject was looked upon with disfavor. Now things have changed. People realize that it is necessary to take a wide as well as a close view. Civilization advances by alternating periods of specialization and generalization. We are now entering upon the second phase.

Then, too, he had come to the conclusion from his study of great scientists that the men who had accomplished most through the prolongation of their productive period had done so by changing their occupation two or three times in the course of their lifetime; for example, Helmholtz, who devoted the first half of his adult life to physiology and medicine and the last to physics, being equally eminent in each; and Humboldt, who kept up his work to the close of his ninety years by shifting from one field of science to another. Having come to this conclusion, Ostwald, as an experimental scientist, was obliged to try it upon himself. The success of the experiment indicates that rotation of crops is a good plan in menticulture as well as agriculture.

He carries out the same principle in his daily life. When tired with philosophizing, he turns to painting. This he finds relieves the mind better than anything else, for it sends the blood to another side of the brain, while if he tries to secure rest by lying down, the brain goes on working in the same old lines. This absorption in artistic effort he has used in his Harvard lecture on "Individuality and Immortality", when he is arguing that the highest happiness is found rather in the obliteration of individuality than its persistence. This conclusion is familiar to us as that of the mystics, but Ostwald reaches it characteristically by another way, the second law of energetics. After speaking of the tendency of liquids and of heat toward diffusion and consequent loss of identity, he applies the principle to society and psychology. The passage is worth quoting because it is practically a direct contradiction of Spencer's fundamental theory that evolution is a progress from homogeneity to heterogeneity, both for matter and for energy. The difference results, I think, chiefly from the fact that Spencer's attention was fixed upon the first law, that of the conservation of energy, for the importance of the second law, that of the dissipation of energy, was not recognized till long afterward.[1] The reader will notice that the second law is decidedly democratic in its implications.

It is a strange thing indeed that by merely being associated with another thing of the same kind identity is lost. And still more strange is the fact that every being of this kind seems driven by an irresistible impulse to seek every occasion for losing its identity. Every known physical fact leads to the conclusion that diffusion, or a homogeneous distribution, of energy is the general aim of all happenings. No change whatever seems to have occurred, and probably none ever will occur, resulting in a concentration greater than the corresponding dissipation of energy. A partial concentration may be brought about in a system, but only at the expense of a greater dissipation, and the sum total is always an increase in dissipation.

While we are as sure as science can make us about the general validity of this law as applied to the physical world, its application to human development may be doubted. It seems to me to hold good in this case also, if it is applied with proper caution. The difficulty lies in the circumstance that we have no exact objective means of measuring homogeneity and heterogeneity in human affairs, and we can therefore not study any given system closely enough to draw a quantitative conclusion. It seems pretty certain that increase of culture tends to diminish the

[1] Spencer laid the foundation of his philosophy in the essay on "Progress: Its Law and Cause" more than twenty years before the publication of Clausius's "Die mechanische Warmetheorie."

differences between men. It equalizes not only the general standard of living, but attenuates also even the natural differences of sex and age. From this point of view I should look upon the accumulation of enormous wealth in the hands of a single man as indicating an imperfect state of culture.

The property which has been described as an irresistible tendency toward diffusion may also be observed in certain cases in man. In conscious beings such natural tendencies are accompanied by a certain feeling which we call will, and we are happy when we are allowed to act according to these tendencies or according to our will. Now, if we recall the happiest moments of our lives, they will be found in every case to be connected with a curious loss of personality. In the happiness of love this fact will be at once discovered. And if you are enjoying intensely a work of art, a symphony of Beethoven's, for example, you find yourself relieved of the burden of personality and carried away by the stream of music as a drop is carried by a wave. The same feeling comes with the grand impressions nature gives us. Even when I am sitting quietly sketching in the open there comes to me in a happy moment a sweet feeling of being united with the nature about me, which is distinctly characterized by complete forgetfulness of my poor self. We may conclude from this that individuality means limitations and unhappiness, or is at least closely connected with them.

Professor Ostwald showed me the studio which now takes the place of the laboratory. It is still part laboratory, for he is experimenting in pigments and has invented new forms of crayons or pastels

and methods of fixation. In painting, as in everything else, he works with rapidity and effectiveness.
Three days at Niagara Falls gave him two dozen
or more pictures. He has a good eye for picturesqueness and uses vivid and varied coloration. He
utilized his time at the University of California to
get some fine views of Berkeley and Professor Loeb's
seaside laboratory. His stay at Harvard as ex-
change professor in 1905 gave him many scenes
from Marblehead and Cambridge, among them a
striking picture of the Harvard stadium seen across
the river flats and looking as imposing as the Coli-
seum. Photography he has practiced from boy-
hood. It was by this and the manufacture of fire-
works in his mother's kitchen that he took his first
steps in chemistry. He has always been fond of
music, both as listener and performer, playing the
violin well, and, says his conscientious biographer, the
bassoon very badly. We are also told that in his
student days he composed a symphony, wrote much
poetry, and applied himself diligently to the study
of the laws of motion by experimenting for hours
on the impact of elastic ivory balls upon a plane
green surface.

Walking, however, has ever been his chief recreation, if we can call that a recreation which is the

means of his most productive thought. After lunch he showed me about his estate, a wooded upland overlooking the village houses, clustered about kirk and *Gasthaus*, and, beyond, the level, orderly Saxon landscape, with its leisurely windmills. The winding walks appear to be sufficiently long to enable him to evolve undisturbed the most complicated German sentence. The stranger can find his way to Landhaus Energie by inquiring of a villager for "the house with the big post box", for when Ostwald took up his residence in Gross-Bothen, this provision had to be made for the enormous mail coming to him from all parts of the world.

One can generally tell in Germany the date of erection or occupancy of a country house by whether it is called a "*Villa*" or a "*Landhaus*." The Germanic movement is bent upon expelling all the foreigners from the language. So now we see *Fahrkarte* in place of *Billet*, formerly used; *Fernsprecher* in place of *Telefon; Zweikampf* in place of *Duell;* and *Einheitslehre* in place of *Monismus.* The adoption of an international auxiliary language would, Professor Ostwald explained to me, facilitate this movement, for it would leave each local language to develop in its own way, free from the penalty of isolation.

WILHELM OSTWALD

I thought, as I walked back through the smooth, clean, tree-lined road to the railroad station, that here at least was a man who had attained that internal peace and happiness, that external honor and usefulness, which theoretically should reward all philosophers. Few men have so wide a fame in science. Still fewer have so many devoted friends among their former students. That he has any personal enemies it would be hard to believe, though he has many opponents. He has earned his success by his own exertions, working his way up to his present position by sheer force of character and ability. He was the second son of a master cooper of Riga, an old Hansa town of Baltic Russia. He was born September 2, 1853, and educated at the *Real-gymnasium* of Riga and the University of Dorpat, Russia (1872–1875). His dissertation at the conclusion of his course here, on "The Mass Action of Water", broke new ground in a field that he was henceforth to make his own. He thought himself lucky then to secure a position as assistant in physics at Dorpat at two hundred and fifty dollars a year, because this gave him an opportunity for research, and his master's and doctor's dissertations attracted attention by their bold adoption and development of the new theories of solutions and affinity.

He utilized his vacations at Riga in cultivating — by means of piano and paint brush —¸the acquaintance of Fräulein Helene von Reyher, whom he married when he was twenty-seven. His comrades reminded him that not long before he had declared that he would never marry, for he should devote all his time to science. But he answered: "I had to marry, because the girl interfered with my work." The measure was efficacious, for she has not interfered with his work since, even finding time to assist in his literary labors, although she has brought up five children. They took their wedding journey in a postwagon from Riga to Dorpat and set up housekeeping with a kerosene stove and a small piano as their principal furniture; no sofa. Readers who understand the importance of the sofa in a German household will appreciate the deprivation. The next year he was called to his native city as professor of chemistry in the Riga Polytechnic, and in 1887 he left Russia for Germany to take the chair of chemistry at Leipzig University.

In his study of men of science Ostwald has introduced the distinction of classicist and romanticist. The classicist keeps to one line of thought and develops it by himself logically and completely. His mind works mathematically, and he is fond of systems and formulation, often addicted to dogmatism. He is accurate and thorough, but deficient in experimental ability and regardless of practical applications. He is reluctant to publish and is apt to be a poor teacher, exerting little personal influence on his students and sometimes none on his contemporaries.

The romanticist, on the other hand, is usually a good teacher and often the founder of a school of thought. He has the expansive temperament and genial disposition; fond of conversation and given to rapid publication. He carries on many different lines of work at the same time and is eager to put them into practice as soon as possible. He is an adventurous theorizer, willing to risk a leap in the dark, arriving at conclusions by a sort of intuition and not always able to explain how he got his results. He is, therefore, liable to make conspicuous mistakes and is apt to be impatient of details. The romanticist gets paid in current coin, that is to say, in the devotion of his disciples and in honors from his colleagues, sometimes even in applause and wealth from a grateful public. The classicist has to put up with deferred payment, and his services to science often receive no adequate recognition until after he is dead and sometimes not then.

Among American scientists we have almost perfect specimens of these two genera. Count Rumford was a typical romanticist and Willard Gibbs a typical classicist, and there was, as I have shown elsewhere,[1] the greatest possible contrast in their characters and careers. Ostwald, it is unnecessary to say, has all the characteristics of the romanticist. He has become a world teacher through his books and periodicals. He has trained in his laboratory Arrhenius, Nernst, and many others of almost equal eminence. He has had the satisfaction of seeing his abstract theories become the working basis of enormous industries.

It is worthy of note that the science which in Germany has been most closely connected with the universities and in which the most pure research has been done, has developed most rapidly and proved most profitable. The annual value of the products of the chemical industries of Germany is over three hundred million dollars. And this is only one of the sources of the new wealth which is coming to Germany and making that country one of the foremost of world powers. In Great Britain emigration exceeds immigration, while in Germany of late the reverse is true, although in Germany the

[1] "Leading American Men of Science." (Holt & Company.)

increase in population from the surplus of births over deaths is nine hundred thousand, twice what it is in Great Britain. At this rate, Germany will soon have a population twice ₄as large as that of Great Britain. And the wealth of Germany is increasing faster than the population, notwithstanding the heavy drains of army and navy. I asked Professor Ostwald the cause of Germany's amazing prosperity. "We Germans believe in science," he answered simply.

The ideals of system, economy, and efficiency which have been developed in the laboratory have been applied in Germany more than elsewhere to military affairs, the promotion of commerce, and methods of administration. That the scientific view should prevail in dealing with all social problems is Ostwald's intent, and in furtherance of this aim he is devoting his chief attention to the discussion of the ethical and political questions of the day through the Monist societies. As an example of his mode of thought on such topics, I quote a passage from his "Individuality and Immortality":

There can be no doubt about nature being full of cruelty. All through the whole realm of organic beings we find in nearly every class of animals and plants some species which live at the expense of their fellow creatures. I mean parasitic organisms of every kind, whether they live in the interior of their hosts, whom they kill or make miserable, or whether they feed directly on other creatures. No one thinks of punishing a cat who tortures a poor mouse for no vital purpose whatever, and we find it perfectly natural that the larvæ of certain wasps should develop in the interior of caterpillars, slowly devouring their hosts from within. It is only man who tries to change this general way of nature's and to diminish as far as possible cruelty and injustice to his fellow man and his fellow creatures. And from the strong desire that this black stain should be removed as fully as possible from humanity, the idea developed that there must be beyond our bodily life a possibility of compensating for the evil which is done and for that which is suffered during life without due punishment or reward as suggested by our sense of justice.

But reward and punishment take on a wholly different aspect when we regard mankind as one collective being. Then the single individual is comparable to a cell in a highly developed organism. Destruction of his fellow cells would be a nuisance and a menace to the whole organism, and therefore any cell which destroyed its neighbors would be either removed from the organism or else encysted and kept from doing further damage. And on the other hand such cells as fulfilled useful purposes would be nourished and protected.

The very necessity for overcoming such dangerous actions on the part of the cells means a decrease in the efficiency of the organism, since the work necessary for the purpose could be better used for the immediate benefit of the organism itself. The best thing would then be to avoid beforehand the formation of such bad cells, and an organism possessed of appropriate means of doing this would have a great advantage.

The application of these considerations to the human collective organism is obvious. Punishment means in every case a loss, and the aim of increasing culture is not to make punishment more effective, but to make it unnecessary. The more each individual is filled with the consciousness that he belongs to the great collective organism of humanity, the less will he be able to separate his own aims and interests from those of humanity. A reconciliation between duty to the race and personal happiness is the result, as well as an unmistakable standard by which to judge our own actions and those of our fellow men.

Self-sacrifice has been considered in all ages and by all religions as the very highest perfection of ethical development. At the same time every man who has thought a little deeper has been aware that the self-sacrifice must have a meaning, that it must result in some effect which could not be attained by other means. Otherwise the self-sacrifice would not be a gain, but rather a loss, to humanity. But we consider self-sacrifice for the sake of humanity as justified, and this corresponds with our general feeling. We admire a man who throws himself into a fire or a torrent to save a child from death; it should mean even more to us when a physician goes into the midst of a raging pestilence conscious of the peril awaiting him. But we do not esteem a man the more for risking his life to save his money from a burning house.

[237]

MAJOR PROPHETS OF TO-DAY

How to Read Ostwald

The only one of Ostwald's philosophical works which is obtainable in English is the "Grundriss der Naturphilosophie", published in Reclam's *Universal-Bibliothek* (Leipzig) and translated by Thomas Seltzer and published by Henry Holt & Company, New York, under the title "Natural Philosophy." This is intended as a succinct popular exposition of the fundamental principles of all the sciences and is mostly devoted to a systematic consideration of the theory of knowledge and laws of logic. It is, therefore, not so interesting to the general reader as some of his untranslated works in which he discusses a variety of ethical and social questions from the scientific standpoint, as for example "Die Forderung des Tages" ("The Day's Demands") (Leipzig: Akademische Verlagsgesellschaft). His "Grosse Männer" (same publisher) contains biographical sketches of Davy, Mayer, Faraday, Liebig, Gerhardt, and Helmholtz as well as his general observations on the character and training of scientific discoverers. Ostwald's Harvard lecture on "Individuality and Immortality" was published by the Houghton, Mifflin Company, 1906. He is now issuing a series of informal talks on scientific ideals and morals under the title of "Monistische Sonntagspredigten" (Verlag des Deutschen Monisten-Bundes in Berlin). A second series was published by the Akademische Verlagsgesellschaft, Leipzig, and a third by the Verlag Unesma, Leipzig. A few of the titles will indicate their character and scope: "Love One Another", "The Jatho Case", "How Evil Came into the World", "The Freedom of the Will", "What is Truth?" "Nietzsche and the Struggle for Existence",

WILHELM OSTWALD

"Natural Science and Paper Science", "The Philosopher's Stone", "Efficiency." The last named was published in *The Independent*, October 19, 1911. "The Wave Theory of History", an explanation of the cause of periodic alternations in finance and politics, was published in *The Independent*, July 10, 1913. An article, "Breaking Barriers", appeared in *The Masses*, February, 1911. It is greatly to be desired that all of these "Monistic Sunday Sermons" as well as "The Day's Duty" and "Great Men" be translated into English, as they represent a point of view of growing importance in modern thought.

Other articles by Ostwald accessible in English are: "The Philosophical Meaning of Energy", in *The International Quarterly*, Vol. VII; "The Modern Theory of Energetics", with criticism by Dr. Carus, in *The Monist*, 1907; "Chemical Energy" in the *Journal of the American Chemical Society*, August, 1893, and in the Smithsonian Report for 1893; "A Contribution to the Theory of Science", his address before the Section of Methodology at the St. Louis Congress, in *Popular Science Monthly*, 1905, p. 219; "The Art of Making Discoveries", in *Science American Supplement*, No. 1807; a character sketch of Sir William Ramsay in *Nature*, January 11, 1912.

Of Ostwald's chemical works the following have been translated into English: "Conversations on Chemistry" (Wiley). "Manual of Physical and Chemical Measurements" (Macmillan), translated by James Walker. "The Scientific Foundation of Analytical Chemistry", translated by G. McGowan (Macmillan). "Solutions", translated by M. Pattison Muir (Longmans). "The Principles of Inorganic Chemistry", translated by Alex. Findlay (Macmillan). "The Fundamental Principles of

[239]

Chemistry", translated by Harry W. Morse (Long-mans). "Letters to a Painter on Theory and Practice", translated by Morse (Ginn). The serious student of Ostwald's thought will of course devote himself chiefly to his "Annalen der Natur- und Kulturphilosophie" (Leipzig: Verlag Unesma). The latest and most complete summary of his conception of the universe is given in "Die Philosophie der Werte" (Alfred Kröner, Leipzig, 1914). In the Lübeck lecture, "Die Ueberwindung des wissenschaftlichen Materialismus" (*Zeitschrift für physikalische Chemie, Band 18*, pp. 305–320, and separately published by Veit, Leipzig, 1895), and the "Vorlesungen über Naturphilosophie" (Veit, 1902) he laid the foundations of his theory. In "Die energetische Grundlagen der Kulturwissenschaft" (Leipzig, 1909) he extended it to include the science of civilization. In "Die wissenschaftliche Stellung" ("Annalen der Naturphilosophie", Vol. X), he defends himself against certain misconceptions, as, for example, that he makes energy the sole reality in the world, or a metaphysical principle like Hartmann's "Unconscious." Ostwald's educational view may be found in chapters of "Die Forderung des Tages", in the article on "The University of the Future and the Future of the University" ("Annalen der Naturphilosophie", Vol. X, p. 236), and in "Wider das Schuleland, Ein Notruf" (Leipzig: Akademische Verlagsgesellschaft). "Erfinder und Entdecker" contains sketches of Mayer, Helmholtz, and Liebig (Vol. XXIV of *Die Gesellschaft*, Frankfurt a. M.: Rütten und Leoning). "Die Energie" is a popular exposition of energetics (Vol. I of Wissen und Können. Leipzig: Barth). Ostwald's contributions to internationalism are mostly published by *Die Brücke*, Munich. His popular propaganda of the gospel of Monism is now carried on by the weekly organ of the society, which he edits, *Das Monistische Jahrhundert* (Verlag Unesma, Leipzig).

An intimate and appreciative sketch of the life and work of "Wilhelm Ostwald" was written by P. Walden on the twenty-fifth anniversary of his doctorate (Leipzig: Engelmann).

There is space here to give only a few references to discussions and criticisms of Ostwald's theories. Doctor Roberty, in "Energétique et Sociologie" (*Revue philosophique*, January, 1910), shows the vast importance of Ostwald's extension of the laws of energetics to vital and social phenomena. A painstaking comparison of the contradictory theories of Lombroso and Ostwald on the character of genius is contributed by Georg Wendel to *Zeit. für Philosophie*, 1910. In the *Vierteljahrsschrift für wiss. Philosophie und Soziologie* for 1905 will be found *Bemerkungen über die Metaphysik in der Ostwald'schen Energetik*, by F. W. Adler, and *Atomistik und Energetik von Standpunkte ökonomischer Naturbetrachtung*, by Hermann Wolff. F. Dennert in his volume on "Die Weltanschauung des modernen Naturforschers" (Stuttgart, 1907) devotes a chapter to Ostwald.

I must also mention the valuable articles contributed by Doctor Fielding H. Garrison to the *New York Medical Journal*, September 11, 1909, on "Physiology and the Second Law of Thermodynamics", in which he discusses the application of the theories of Gibbs and Ostwald to biology.

CHAPTER VI

ERNST HAECKEL

Monistic investigation of nature as knowledge of the true, monistic ethic as training for the good, monistic æsthetic as pursuit of the beautiful — these are the three great departments of our monism : by the harmonious and consistent cultivation of these we effect at last the truly beatific union of religion and science so painfully longed for by so many to-day. The True, the Beautiful, the Good, these are the three august Divine Ones before which we bow the knee in adoration ; in the unforced combination and mutual supplementing of these we gain the pure idea of God. To this triune Divine Ideal shall the twentieth century build its altars. — Haeckel's "The Confession of Faith of a Man of Science."

THE geographical distribution of German universities is such as to shock the orderly mind of our General Education Board, which, like a trained forester, believes in weeding out, or rather, in not cultivating, institutions growing close together. But in Germany the soil is so rich as to support three great universities — Leipzig, Halle, and Jena — planted within a circle of twenty miles radius, and nevertheless all thriving. Even the overweening development of Berlin University since that city has become the imperial capital has not yet over-shadowed the smaller institutions. For, curious as it seems to us Americans, students in Europe are not influenced in the choice of a university chiefly by its size, the splendor of its buildings, or even its athletic record. They seem rather to consider the personality of the professors as the important thing, and will often travel considerable distances, at a cost of one and sixteen hundredths cents per mile, third class, in order to put themselves under the instruction of a particular man they have taken a fancy to, quite ignoring some other university which from our point of view had a claim upon their allegiance, from the fact that it was nearer or had been attended by their fathers. Jena, the least of the three in the matter of numbers, is not by reason of that willing to confess inferiority to any of its rivals, not even to big Berlin. On the contrary, Haeckel, in his famous controversy with Virchow, apologized with satirical politeness for his opponent's ignorance of zoölogy, on the ground that he could not be expected to keep up with the advance of the science when he had left the little institute of Würzburg for the luxurious appliances and the political and social duties of Berlin. In fact, Haeckel, with his fondness for formulation,

[243]

laid down a law on this point thirty-five years ago which, he says, has yet to meet with contradiction, that "the scientific work of an institution stands in inverse ratio to its size."

Certainly, if seclusion and scholarly traditions are conducive to intellectual achievement, Jena is the place for the thinker. The university, with one thousand eight hundred and seventeen students, is about a third the size of the University of Wisconsin. The population of the city is about the same as that of Madison. But while Madison has other interests, political especially, Jena is absorbed in the university. Its chief industry, the glassworks, is the offspring of the university, for it was through the fortunate collaboration of Ernst Abbé, a professor who could figure out indices of refraction, with Carl Zeiss, a glassmaker who was willing to put money into queer formulas, that the new lenses were discovered which make possible our modern photography and microscopy. Generously has the debt that the industry owed to science been repaid, for the Zeiss company has borne a large share of the expenses of maintaining the university and erecting its new buildings, besides giving to the city many public buildings, among them a splendid bathhouse, an auditorium and a free library and reading room, where are on file one hundred and fifteen daily papers and three hundred and sixty periodicals (American librarians, take notice).

From this it may be seen that Jena is an up-to-date town. Yet at the same time it retains more of medieval picturesqueness than most, mingling the new and the old as none but Germans know how to. "*Das liebe närrische Nest,*" as Goethe called it, is hidden away among the Thuringian hills so that the railroad was a long time finding it. The cobble-stoned streets stroll out from the market place in a casual sort of a way and change their minds about where they are going without notice, twisting about Gothic churches, diving under old towers, wandering slowly along the banks of the Saale, or starting suddenly straight up hill. The gossipy gables of the old houses lean toward each other like peaked eldritch faces in fluted red caps. So close they stand sometimes that you can touch the walls on either side, and you have to walk with one foot on the sidewalk and the other on the pavement, like the absent-minded German professor who thought he had gone lame. When I saw Jena, I understood something which had long puzzled me, that is, how the dachshund originated. It is manifestly a product of evolution according to the principle of the survival of the

[245]

fittest, for only a creature constructed according to
the specifications "dog and a half long and half a
dog high" could make his way with convenience and
celerity through this maze of narrow streets. But all
sorts of vehicles and beasts of burden get around
somehow, too; oxen and horses, automobiles and
bicycles, dog carts and women carts. Most in evidence everywhere are the students, who swagger
through the town with the consciousness of owning it,
their bright-colored corps caps at a cocky angle, and
their faces looking like advertisements of the dangers
of not using safety razors, for the Jena student has
three hundred and fifty years of university tradition
to live up to, and he realizes the responsibility of it
to the full.

The ancient and honorable history of Jena is
unescapable. It is woven into the very fabric of the
place, and he who runs may read it from the street
signs. The Volkshaus, which I have mentioned, is
very appropriately approached through Ernst Abbé
Strasse and Carl Zeiss Strasse. On the other side
of it is Luther Strasse, for Jena harbored the great
reformer for two years at a critical period in his
career. This leads to Goethe Strasse — Goethe
composed the "Erlkönig" at Jena. The next turn
brings us into Schiller Strasse — Schiller was pro-

fessor of history in the University for ten years, carrying an active side line of poetry the while. A big stone in the old garden marks the spot where he wrote "Wallenstein," 1798. At the garden gate is Ernst Haeckel Platz, from which Ernst Haeckel Strasse leads us to our destination, the Villa Medusa. What other town could give a ten-minute walk so rich in names worth remembering?

The Villa Medusa, mind you, is not named from the Greek gorgon, but from the beautiful jellyfish with the long trail of waving threads, one of the living comets dredged up by the *Challenger* which Haeckel depicted and described thirty years ago. The house is a square-built, white, two-story dwelling, half hidden by the tall trees. The furniture is of the conventional German type. The room into which I was shown was not small, but it seemed so when Professor Haeckel entered it, for the first impression one gets is largeness. He really is a large man any way you take him; tall, heavy-limbed, large-featured; his hair is now white but thick, and his beard broad and bushy. He moves with some stiffness now, but otherwise his fourscore years have not impaired his vigor. His bearing is erect and his handclasp strong. His laugh is hearty and his blue eyes twinkle as he relates some amusing incident in the controversies of which his life has been full.

For Haeckel has been a storm center of the cyclonic movements that have swept over the whole earth during the last century. His name has been a battle-cry in the scientific, religious, and political wars of more than one generation, and never more than at present, when a new religion with many thousands of adherents has set out to conquer the world under the sign, "There is one Substance and Haeckel is its prophet." I inferred from what he said to me and still more from what he did not say that he was not very enthusiastic over the semi-ecclesiastical form which the propaganda is now taking in Germany, but is more interested in the quieter and wider acceptance of his ideas which he regards as virtually complete in scientific circles. He disclaimed emphatically any intention of establishing a cult or ritual, like Comte. I fancy that the sentence with which he ended his chapter on "Our Monistic Religion",

Just as the Catholics had to relinquish a number of churches to the Reformation in the sixteenth century, so a still larger number will pass over to the free societies of Monists in the coming years,

was, like many another paragraph in the book, put in more to irritate the clergy than with any serious

Ernst Haeckel

intent. But it is curious to observe how rapidly the Monist locals are assuming the forms of the non-conformist congregations. They celebrate Christmas — that is, the winter solstice — with trees, candles, and gifts. They have a weekly sermon by Ostwald and a Sunday-school paper, *Die Sonne*.

To see Haeckel at his best one should get him to talk of his beloved Jena, which indeed is not difficult to do, for he is ever ready to speak with enthusiasm of its beauty, its freedom of thought, and its leadership in many of the great intellectual movements of German history. When I remarked upon the many delightful roads and pathways upon the hills round about the town, he explained Jena was the last of the university towns to be reached by railroad. Professors and students were poor, and they had to walk, so they learned to walk well and to take pleasure in outdoor exercise and to appreciate fine views. That Haeckel himself is a great lover of landscape as well as of the beautiful in all forms of life is well known to readers of his travel sketches. For this he gives credit to his mother, who, as he says in dedicating to her his "Indian Letters",

Aroused in me in my earliest childhood a sense for the infinite beauty of nature and taught the growing boy the value of time and the joy of labor.

His skill as a draftsman and colorist appears in his zoölogical works, and besides this professional work he has in his portfolios more than a thousand original sketches in oil and water colors of scenery from Norway to Malay; in fact, of every quarter of the globe except America. When he was twenty-five he was so captivated by Sicily that he almost gave up science to adopt landscape painting as a career.

The freedom of instruction which Jena has enjoyed to an exceptional degree, even for Germany, Haeckel ascribes in part to the fact that the university is located in one of the minor States, remote from the great political centers, and derives its support from several sources. "We had four masters," said Professor Haeckel to me, "and so we remained free." He closes his address of 1892 on "Monism as the Bond Between Religion and Science" with a grateful eulogy of the Grand Duke Karl Alexander, who, he says,

has during a prosperous reign of forty years constantly shown himself an illustrious patron of science and art; as Rector Magnificentissimus of our Thuringian university of Jena, he has always afforded his protection to its most sacred palladium — the right of free investigation and the teaching of truth.

We see that Haeckel has reason to be grateful for the protection accorded him when we realize that he

first championed the cause of Darwin in 1862, only
three years after the publication of "The Origin of
Species", and that twenty years after that professors
were being dismissed from American universities or
were viewed with suspicion for believing in evolution.
Even to-day a man of Haeckel's views on religion and
his blunt way of expressing them would find it difficult to retain his chair in most American universities.
In Germany a professor may be almost anything he
pleases — except a Socialist — and hold his job.

A song of the Jena students contains the couplet

"Wer die Wahrheit kennet und saget sie nicht,
Der ist fürwahr ein erbärmlicher Wicht!"

But according to Haeckel the students of Berlin
University have a different version:

Wer die Wahrheit kennet und saget sie frei,
Der kommt in Berlin auf die Stadtvogtei![1]

The grand duchy of Saxe-Weimar-Eisenach, of
which Jena is one of the chief cities, has about the
same area as Rhode Island and fewer inhabitants.
It was the first of the German States to acquire a

---

[1] An undergraduate friend of mine to whom I referred these verses for
translation into the vernacular of the campus gives me this version:

Who knows the truth and speaks not out
He is indeed a sorry lout!
Who knows the truth and speaks too loose
In Berlin gets in the calaboose!

constitutional government, in 1816. The community is rather rigidly orthodox in the evangelical Lutheran faith, which it was among the first to espouse. How well the Grand Duke Karl Alexander maintained the Jena tradition of *Lehrfreiheit* is shown by an incident that happened when Haeckel first scandalized Germany by championing the cause of Darwinism. A prominent theologian came to the palace of the Grand Duke at Weimar and begged him to dismiss the heretic professor. Karl Alexander asked: "Do you suppose that he really believes the things he publishes?"

"Most certainly he does," was the prompt reply.

"Very well," said the Grand Duke, "then the man simply does the same as you do."

It was about this time, when Haeckel, perceiving that the University was suffering from the attack made upon him, approached Seebeck, the head of the governing body, with an offer to resign his professorship in order to relieve the tension. Seebeck, who had little sympathy with his theories, replied: "My dear Haeckel, you are still young and you will come yet to have more mature views of life. After all, you will do less harm here than elsewhere, so you had better stay."

It may be well to add that while Haeckel did not

change his views except to become more radical as he grew older, the University did not suffer in the long run by his presence. On the contrary, his fame as an investigator and teacher drew students from all over the world and brought to the University several large endowments.

Near to Ernst Haeckel Strasse and facing the park called Paradise there is a unique building, the Phyletic Museum, established by Haeckel to house collections illustrating the theory of evolution. On the wall is painted the genealogical tree of the greatest family in the world, embracing the whole animal kingdom, and over the central arch is inscribed a quotation from the poet whom Haeckel most admires, Goethe:

> Wer Wissenschaft und Kunst besitzt
>   Der hat Religion;
> Wer diese beiden nicht besitzt
>   Der habe Religion!

Which Lange puts into English as

> He who Science has and Art
>   He has Religion too;
> Let him who in these has no part
>   Make his religion do.

Nowadays, when evolution is generally accepted, when it is preached from the pulpit as well as taught in the school, it is hard for us to realize the scorn and incredulity that greeted the theory on its first formulation. We who see about us laboratories of experimental evolution where new species of plants and animals are produced at will, according to specifications drawn up in advance, can hardly put ourselves in the position of those who fifty years ago believed that to question the immutability of species was to induce intellectual confusion and invite moral chaos. So we can scarcely appreciate the courage and perspicacity of the young Haeckel in openly championing Darwinism at a time when that theory was regarded as an absurdity, not alone by theologians, as one would infer from Andrew D. White's "Warfare of Science with Theology", but by most of the leading authorities in all fields of science. But we may picture him on that memorable Sunday evening of September 19, 1863, as he rose to give the opening address of the Scientific Congress at Stettin ; a tall, handsome young man, blond-bearded, bright-eyed, sun-browned, hard-working, athletic (that same year he won a laurel crown at the Leipzig festival for a record-breaking jump of twenty feet). It was certainly presumptuous in a zoölogist of only twenty-nine years, who had just secured a position in the university circle as Extraordinary Professor at Jena (which means below the Ordinary in Germany); who had just published his first book, the "Monograph on the Radiolaria", so to attack the convictions of his elders and masters there assembled. Haeckel was no halfway man. As soon as he espoused Darwinism — which was barely a month after he had laid eyes on "The Origin of Species" — he drew from it conclusions that Darwin himself hesitated to suggest; on the one hand that life originated in inorganic matter, on the other that the human race originated from the lower animals. He at once drew up a pedigree not only of the radiolaria but of mankind. Here is a passage from the very beginning of his Stettin speech:

As regards man himself, if we are consistent we must recognize his immediate ancestors in the ape-like mammals; earlier still in kangaroo-like marsupials; beyond these, in the secondary period, in lizard-like reptiles; and finally, at a yet earlier stage, the primary period, in lowly organized fishes.

and this, be it remembered, was eight years before Darwin published his "Descent of Man."

"Without Haeckel there would have been Darwin, but no Darwinism," says one of his enthusiastic disciples. But this immediately suggests the question of whether it was altogether an advantage to have made an "ism" out of Darwin. As a mere question of taxonomy his theory would have been regarded by the lay world as harmless and uninteresting. But heralded by Haeckel as evidential of materialism, as antagonistic to the Church and as destructive to Christianity, Darwinism raised up foes on all sides who would not otherwise have concerned themselves with it. This, however, is a question of what-might-have-been like to that of whether the slaves might not have been freed without bloodshed *if* the abolitionists had not been so extreme and if the Southerners had not been so intolerant. So in this case; Haeckel was extreme, his opponents were intolerant, so the war had to be. The gentle-natured Darwin more than once had to caution his ardent German champion to be less violent and sweeping in his attacks upon those who held the older views. They were more to be pitied than blamed, said Darwin, and they could not keep back permanently the stream of truth. In England Huxley at the same time, with quite as sharp a pen as Haeckel's, was waging a similar warfare against clerical antagonists.

It may be said that Haeckel spent the rest of his life in filling in the outline he had sketched at the Stettin Congress of 1863, for, however detailed the work on which he was engaged, he never afterward lost sight of the guiding clew to the labyrinth of life evolution. We are here not concerned with the zoölogical studies on which his fame securely rests, but only with the philosophical views to which they led him. His convictions were very definitely established in early manhood, and he occupies to-day essentially the same point of view as fifty years ago. During this time his efforts have been increasingly directed toward reaching a wider audience. In 1866 he developed the fundamental principles of his monistic philosophy in the two large volumes of his "General Morphology of Organisms." This gained few readers outside the circle of savants, and little acceptance there. In 1868 he put his theory of evolution into more popular form in "The Natural History of Creation." This had an unusual sale for a book of its kind, but Haeckel was dissatisfied to see that the general public remained indifferent and unaffected by the new conceptions of the world and man arising from the discoveries of modern science. Worse still, he observed with alarm a rising tide of reactionary thought at the close of the century and a growing dominance of the clerical power in German politics. So he determined to make a final effort to influence his generation, an appeal to the court of last resort, the Cæsar of to-day, the people. He packed his science and philosophy into one volume of moderate size, filled in the chinks with *obiter dicta*, and published it in 1899 under the title of "The Riddle of the Universe." This time he hit the mark. The success of the book was immediate and amazing. An author of a detective tale or a Zenda romance might have envied him. Ten thousand copies were sold within a few months, one hundred thousand within a year, and by this time the sale of the German and English editions has doubtless passed the half million mark, not to speak of the fourteen other languages into which the book has been translated. Since a book like this usually has several readers for each copy, it is probable that those who have been directly reached by Haeckel within fifteen years must be numbered by the million. Besides this, of course, the spread of his views has been further extended by a similar volume, "The Wonders of Life", five years later, and by the widely circulated pamphlets of the Deutscher Monistenbund. *Haeckels einheitliche Weltanschauung*,[1] then, whatever one may think of it, is undeniably an important factor in the thought of to-day.

I found Professor Haeckel not altogether pleased that he owed his popular reputation to that one of his

[1] This is *not* to be translated, as I once heard a student give it, "Haeckel's one-sided showing-up of the universe."

works in which he took the least pride. He seemed
to hold it in almost as light esteem as his opponents
and was frank in acknowledging its defects of style
and content. "But," he said in substance to me,
"I had set forth my philosophy with due dignity and
order in my 'General Morphology' more than thirty
years before and nobody read it. Nobody reads it
now, even when they criticize my ideas. So what
could I do but put them forth in a way that would
secure attention?"

We must observe that to secure this wider audience
he did not resort to any of the ordinary expedients,
such as palliating unpopular views, skipping dry
details, and avoiding technical terms. "The Riddle
of the Universe" is not the sort of writing that goes
by the name of "popular science" and that is commonly regarded as necessary to catch the attention
and reach the understanding of the lay reader.
Haeckel discusses questions of physiology, zoölogy,
botany, paleontology, and astronomy, each in its
own tongue, the bare facts stated without any poetic
disguise or flowery adornment. Far from dodging
long words when necessary, he invents them when
unnecessary. Few men have done so much word
coinage. In his work on the radiolaria alone he had
to christen more than thirty-five hundred new

species, two names apiece. So it is no wonder that when he comes to talking metaphysics and religion he sticks to the habit of making up his language as he goes.

In the case of other authors of this series I have had to distill the essence of their philosophy from the leaves of many volumes. I have had sometimes to translate poetry into prose and sometimes to piece together scattered suggestions and faint allusions into a coherent and compact doctrine. But in the case of Haeckel my task is easy, for nothing of the sort is necessary. He has himself expressed his views in succinct form and the plainest of language. He takes as much delight in creeds and dogmatic statements as any scholastic theologian, and he has the same implicit faith in formulas as capable of expressing all things in heaven and earth. One reason why his conflicts with the clergy have been so sharp and bitter is because he has much the same type of mind and uses similar language. Ordinarily, in the so-called warfare of religion and science, the adversaries revolve hopelessly around one another, like double stars, without ever coming into contact.

The most convenient formulation of Haeckel's philosophy for our purpose is that which he prepared as a sort of confession of faith for his lay church, the

Monistenbund. It is here translated entire and for the most part literally, though in a somewhat condensed form.[1]

THE THIRTY THESES OF MONISM

I. — *Theoretical Monism*

1. Monistic Philosophy. The unitary conception of the world is based solely upon the solid ground of scientific knowledge acquired by human reason through critical experience.

2. Empiricism. This empirical knowledge is attained partly by sense observations on the external world and partly by conscious reflection on our mental internal world.

3. Revelation. In opposition to this monistic theory of knowledge is the prevailing dualistic conception of the world, that the most profound and important truths can be gained through supernatural or divine revelation. All such ideas are due either to obscure and uncritical dogmas or pious frauds.

4. Apriorism. Equally untenable is the assertion of Kantian metaphysics that some knowledge is acquired *a priori* independent of any experience.

5. Cosmological Monism. The world is one great whole, a cosmos, ruled by fixed laws.

6. Cosmological Dualism. The idea that there are two worlds, one material or natural and the other spiritual or supernatural, arises from ignorance, cloudy thinking, and mystical tradition.

7. Biophysics. Biology is only a part of the all-

[1] "Thesen zur Organization des Monism."

embracing physical science and living beings are under the same laws as inorganic matter.

8. Vitalism. The so-called "vital force", which is still believed by some to direct and control physical and chemical processes in the organism, is just as fictitious as a "cosmical intelligence."

9. Genesis. Organic beings and inorganic nature alike have been developed by one great process of evolution through an unbroken chain of transformations causally connected. Part of this universal process of evolution is directly perceptible; its beginning and end are unknown to us.

10. Creation. The idea that a personal creator made the world out of nothing and embodied his creative thought in the form of organisms must be abandoned. Such an anthropomorphic creator exists as little as does a "moral world order" ordained by him or a "divine providence."

11. Theory of Descent. That all existing beings are the transformed descendants of a long series of extinct organisms developed in the course of millions of years is proved by comparative anatomy, ontogeny, and paleontology. This biogenetic transformation is established whether we explain it by selection, mutation, or any other theory.

12. Archigony. When the earth's crust had cooled sufficiently, organic life came into existence through the katalysis of colloidal compounds of carbon and nitrogen in the form of structureless plasma globules (Monera) represented to-day by the Chromoceæ.

13. Plasmic Metabolism. The innumerable forms of plant and animal life arose from the ceaseless transformation of the living substance in which the most important factors are the physiological functions of variation and heredity.

14. Phylogeny. All plants and animals form a single genealogical tree rooted in the Monera.

15. Anthropogeny. The position of man in nature is now fully understood. He has all the characteristics of the vertebrates and mammals and developed out of this class in the later tertiary period.

16. Pithecoid Theory. Man is most nearly related to the tailless apes, but is not descended from any of the existing forms. On the contrary, the common ancestors of all the anthropoid apes and man are to be looked for in the earlier extinct species of old world apes (Pithecanthropus).

17. Athanism. The soul consists of the totality of cerebral functions. This soul or thought organ in man, a certain area of the cerebral cortex, acts in accordance with the same laws of psychophysics as in the other mammals. This function of course ceases at death, so it is nowadays utterly absurd to believe in "the personal immortality of the soul."

18. Indeterminism. The human will, like all other functions of the brain (sensation, imagination, ratiocination), is dependent upon the anatomy of this organ and is necessarily determined by the inherited and acquired characteristics of the individual brain. The old doctrine of "free will" is therefore seen to be untenable and must give way to the opposite doctrine of determinism.

19. God. If by this ambiguous term is understood a personal "Supreme Being", a ruler of the cosmos who, after the manner of men, thinks, loves, generates, rules, rewards, punishes, etc., such an anthropomorphic God must be relegated to the realm of the mystical fiction, no matter whether this personal God be invested with a human form or regarded as an invisible spirit or as a "gaseous

vertebrate." For modern science the idea of God is tenable only so far as we recognize in this "God" the ultimate unknowable cause of things, the unconscious hypothetical "first cause of substance."

20. Law of Substance. The older chemical law of the conservation of matter (Lavoisier, 1789) and the more recent physical law of the conservation of energy (Mayer, 1842) were later (1892) by our Monism united into a single great universal law, for we recognized matter and energy (body and spirit) as inseparable attributes of substance (Spinoza).

II. — *Practical Monism*

21. Sociology. The culture which has raised the human race high above the other animals and given it dominion over the earth depends upon the rational coöperation of men in society with a thoroughgoing division of labor and the mutual interdependence of the laboring classes. The biological foundations of society are already perceptible among the gregarious animals (especially the primates). Their herds and groups are kept together by the social instinct (hereditary habits).

22. Constitution and Laws. The rational arrangement of society and its regulation by laws can be attained by various forms of government, the chief object of which is a just Nomocracy, the establishment of a secular power based upon justice. The laws which limit the freedom of the citizen for the good of society should be based solely upon the national application of natural science, not upon venerable tradition (inherited habits).

23. Church and Creed. On the other hand, all means should be used to fight the hierarchy which

cloaks the secular power with a spiritual mantle and makes use of the credulity of the ignorant masses to further its selfish aims. The confessional obligation as a particular form of superstition is especially to be attacked, since it only serves to evoke the distinction between those of other beliefs. The desirable separation of Church and State is to be accomplished in such a way that the State leaves equally free all forms of belief while restricting their practical encroachments. The spiritual power (Theocracy) must always be subordinate to the secular government (Nomocracy).

24. Papistry. The strongest hierarchy which today exercises spiritual domination over the greater part of the civilized world is papistry or ultramontanism. Although this mighty political organization stands in sharp contradiction with the original pure form of Christianity and wrongfully employs its insignia to obtain power, it nevertheless finds strong support even from its natural opponents, the secular princes. In the inevitable *Kulturkampf* against papistry it is, above all, necessary to abrogate by law its three strongest supports, the celibacy of the clergy, auricular confession, and the sale of indulgences. These three dangerous and immoral institutions of the neo-Catholic church are foreign to original Christianity. So also is the strengthening of superstitions dangerous to society through the cult of miracles (Lourdes, Marpingen) and of relics (Aix la Chapelle, Trèves) to be prevented by law.

25. Monistic Religion. If we understand by religion, not a superstitious cult and irrational creed, but the elevation of the mind through the noblest gifts of art and science, then Monism forms a "bond between religion and science" (1892). The three ideals of this rational monistic religion are truth,

virtue, and beauty. In all civilized states it is the duty of the representatives of the people to see that the monistic religion is officially recognized and its equal rights with other confessions assured.

26. Monistic Ethics. The rational ethics which forms a part of this monistic religion is derived, according to our modern theory of evolution, from the social instincts of the higher animals, not from a dogmatic "categorical imperative" (Kant). Like all of the higher gregarious animals, man strives to attain the natural equilibrium between the two different obligations, the behest of egoism and the behest of altruism. The ethical principle of the "Golden Rule" has expressed this double obligation twenty-five hundred years ago in the maxim: "Do unto others as you would that they should do unto you."

27. Monistic Schools. In most civilized countries, and especially in Germany, the instruction of youth in upper and lower grades is still largely bound in fetters which the scholastic tradition of the Middle Ages has retained to the present day. Only the complete separation of Church and school can loose these fetters. The prevailing confessional or dogmatic religious instruction is to be replaced by comparative religious history and monistic ethics. The influence of the clergy of any confession is to be removed from the school. The inevitable school reform must be accomplished upon the basis of modern natural science. The greater part of education should be devoted, not to the study of the classical language and history, but to the various branches of natural science, especially anthropology and evolution.

28. Monistic Education. Since the sound development of the soul (as a function of the cerebral

cortex) is closely connected with that of the rest of the organism, the monistic education of youth, free from the dogmatic teachings of the Church, must strive to upbuild soul and body equally from earliest youth. Daily gymnastics, baths and exercises, walks and tours, must develop and strengthen the organism from early youth. Observation and love of nature will be thus awakened and intensified. Through public libraries, continuation schools, and popular monistic lectures will the more advanced be provided with mental nourishment.

29. Monistic Culture. The admirable height of culture which mankind in the nineteenth century has attained, the astonishing progress of science and its practical applications in technology, industry, medicine, etc., gives grounds for expecting a still greater development of culture in the twentieth century. This desirable progress will then however be possible only if the beaten paths of the traditional dogmas and of clerical superstition be abandoned and a rational monistic knowledge of nature attain the mastery instead.

30. The Monistenbund. In order to spread the natural unitary theory of the universe to the widest circles and to realize practically the beneficent fruits of theoretical monism, it is desirable that all efforts in this direction find a common point of application through the founding of individual monist societies. In this universal monist association not only all free thinkers and all adherents of the monistic philosophy find place, but also free congregations, ethical societies, and free religious associations, etc., which recognize pure reason as the only rule of their thought and action and not belief in traditional dogma and pretended revelations.

[267]

There is a strong resemblance in form between this creed of the monistic religion and the creeds that have been formulated by many other religions in the history of the world; the same juxtaposition of cosmogony and ethics without any apparent connection; the same mixture of the fundamental and trivial, the permanent and ephemeral; the same affirmation of idealistic aims mingled with attacks upon what is assumed to be the beliefs of the opposition.

It is not my purpose in this book to criticize the views I present or to obtrude my personal opinions, so I shall not discuss this monistic confession of faith except to point out the striking contrast between the theoretical and practical sections of the statement. The second is in no sense a deduction from the first, and they are so different in character as to give the effect of an anticlimax. Haeckel's fundamental principles are bold and revolutionary. His practical conclusions are timid and conventional. It would be a dull faculty meeting which did not bring out more heretical views on education than Haeckel expresses. Why is it necessary to storm the battlements of heaven and create a new earth in order to make Greek optional and get the students to take baths and walks?[1] Any session of the American Socio-

[1] "Riddle of the Universe", p. 363.

logical Society will bring out more suggestions for the radical reorganization of society from professors in good and regular standing than are to be found in all of Haeckel's works. He seems blind to what would appear to us the glaring evils of his country, the burden of militarism, the oppression of government, the conflict of classes, the monopoly of land, the injustice of hereditary rank, the superstition of royalty, and the like. If he touches on these at all, it is in mild and cautious terms. His gratitude to the Grand Duke who was kind enough to let him alone is expressed in language that sounds sycophantic to American ears. All his fury is directed against the Church, Protestant and Catholic alike, yet he remained until the age of seventy-seven a member of the orthodox Lutheran Church. Of course, to be radical in thought and conventional in practice is not peculiar to Haeckel. It is common to most thinkers, but is especially conspicuous in his case.

The reforms he advocates in social customs are for the most part very moderate. He is himself no smoker, and he thinks that the German students devote too much attention to beer and dueling. This is sensible but not startling. He declaims against the tyranny of fashion and denounces corsets as

injurious to the health.[1]   In this, however, most men
and not a few women would agree with him.   He
asserts that marriage is not a sacrament, but a civil
contract, and as such may be dissolved[2].   This is a
doctrine common to Hebrew and Puritan.   One of
the chief objects of the founding of the Monistenbund
was to force the separation of Church and State and
the secularization of the schools.   This seems so
obviously just and desirable that it is hard for us to
realize on what grounds it should be opposed.   And
as for the demands expressed in Article 25 it is
almost inconceivable to us that a government could
refuse a man the right to declare himself a Monist,
instead of a Lutheran or a Hebrew, if he wants to.

In our own free land anybody can get up a church
of his own if he find disciples, and if he prefers to
belong to no church it is nobody's business but his
own.   Not so in Germany, where a man has to give
his religion together with his age and occupation at
every turn.   Even if he wants nothing more than a
permit to a building or a rebate on his railroad fare,
he is called upon to make a confession of faith.   And
it must be one of the few religions officially recognized by the State; none of the "fancy religions"
will pass muster.   A man who declares himself not a

---

[1] "Wonders of Life", p. 430.   [2] *Ibid.*, p. 248.

member of an established church, *konfessionslos*, is looked upon with suspicion as a sort of outlaw. Under these circumstances, of course, a large proportion of the adherents of the State churches never attend the services and have no belief in the creed they profess.

There is now going on in Germany what might be called an "anti-Christian revival." Protracted meetings are being held in the cities at which Monist missionaries exhort the people to leave the Church, and at the conclusion the converts are called upon to stand up and be counted. In 1913, during a whirlwind campaign in Berlin at Christmas time, sixteen meetings were held and attended by thirteen thousand persons, of whom twenty-three hundred and forty-three announced their intention of formally separating themselves from the churches of which they are nominally members. The Monist locals, the independent congregations, and the free-thinker societies have joined forces under the management of a central *Komitee Konfessionslos*. Very curiously the Social Democratic party, which in its early days was so fiercely anti-clerical, stands aloof from the movement and appears to view it with disfavor.

This *Kirchenaustrittsbewegung*, or church-exit-movement has for its aim to effect the complete separation of Church and State and to secure for the individual freedom of religious choice. It does not, therefore, indicate so great an increase of irreligion as appears on the face of it. It will on the contrary tend to reduce the percentage of hypocrisy and to allow the growth of new forms of religious association better adapted to the times than the established churches. Already it has stimulated a useful reflex. The "Go-to-church Sunday" has been introduced from America, and the State churches are showing more signs of life than for a long time.

It would obviously be an injustice to Haeckel to assume that, because the practical reforms he advocates seem trite and timid to us, they do not require both perspicacity and courage in Germany. The fact is that Germany, advanced though it be intellectually, is still medieval in government and usages. If, for instance, a German clergyman should visit this country and stay in the home of an American minister, the latter would probably be distressed by the views held by the visitor on the inerrancy of the Scriptures and the value of beer, while, on the other hand, the German would be equally shocked to hear his reverend friend advocate secular schools and ridicule the divine right of kings.

ERNST HAECKEL

Haeckel practically takes over intact the fundamental principles of Christian ethics, making the Golden Rule the basis of his system, although characteristically refusing to give Jesus any credit for it by saying that it had a "polyphyletic origin." He attacks, indeed, certain extreme forms of it, asceticism, belittlement of family life, absolute self-sacrifice, etc., but he adopts substantially the moral standards which the Christian men of his time and environment profess and endeavor to practice. I do not say that he is wrong to borrow ethics from Christianity. I do not suppose he could do better. But he would have done the world great service if, instead of taking a ready-made ethical system, he had worked it out from his fundamental principle of evolution, as Spencer, Drummond, and Kropotkin have tried to do. If, having done this, he had arrived at the same conclusions as the Christian moralists, his aid would have been invaluable just now, when, almost for the first time, attacks are made not so much on the theology as on the ethics of Christianity, and this, too, in the name of science. The air is filled with questions which arise in Haeckel's peculiar field. Is, for example, Nietzsche justified in preaching ruthless egoism as the logical lesson of evolution ? Or is it true, as many now say, that the

[273]

preservation and protection of the weak in body and mind necessarily lead to the degeneration of the race? In the incidental references he makes to these questions,[1] he condemns Nietzsche, but advocates euthanasia for the hopelessly diseased, reaching the first conclusion from his "own personal opinion" and the second from "pure reason." As the individual views of an evolutionist, these are interesting and even valuable, but they can hardly be regarded as established principles of the science of evolutionary ethics.

Haeckel's politics may be summed up by saying that he is anti-clerical and not much else. He concerns himself little about the form of government or economic conditions, regarding them indeed as comparatively unimportant matters.

The monistic and the socialistic movements in Germany are closely associated, but chiefly, it seems to me, because both are anti-clerical rather than because the evolutionary philosophy necessarily leads to either democracy or socialism. Many Social Democrats profess themselves Monists, and doubtless a large proportion of that party would agree with Haeckel in the matter of religion. But on the other hand, they can derive little if any support for their

[1] "Wonders of Life", pp. 115 and 119.

doctrines from the monistic literature. Haeckel states his opinion with his usual frankness in a contribution to Maximilian Harden's magazine, which concludes with the words:

I am certainly no friend of Herr Bebel, who has attacked me repeatedly, and among other things has slandered me in his book ʃon Woman. Besides, I hold the utopian aims of the official social democracy to be impracticable and its ideal future state to be a big workhouse. That, however, cannot prevent me from recognizing the kernel of justice in the great social movement. That this can be overcome by the repressive acts of the Berlin council, by the power of the police and of the State prosecutors can be believed only by one who knows neither the history nor the natural history of mankind. — *Zukunft*, 1895, No. 18. Quoted in the introduction to "Freie Wissenschaft und freie Lehre", p. 9.

The immense popularity of "The Riddle of the Universe" is, I think, largely to be accounted for by the personality of the author. The man behind the gun was what gave it power. I do not mean that the reception given to the book was due to Haeckel's standing as a zoölogist. The outside world knows little and cares less for scientific reputation. It was rather that the boc l revealed a man tremendously in earnest who had made up his mind on questions of the most vital interest to all and who said what he thought in the plainest and most emphatic language, without regard to whose feelings he hurt. "The Riddle of the Universe" and "The Wonders of Life" are, it seems to me, more valuable as contributions to the psychology of genius than to philosophy. The personal interest he aroused is evinced by the thousands of letters he received and is still receiving about these books, ranging in tone from the warmly sympathetic to the furiously antagonistic. He years ago had to give up the task of answering them save by a printed slip.

Few books have ever excited so much heated controversy. Hundreds of criticisms and replies have been published, and new ones appear frequently yet, fifteen years after. The book was intended to draw the fire of the enemy, clericalism, and it did. Nor did the philosophy of the chair receive it any more favorably. It will be sufficient on this point to quote the sharp criticism of Professor Friedrich Paulsen, of Berlin University, whose idealistic monism comes into direct contact with Haeckel's materialistic monism:

"I have read this book with burning shame for the state of general culture and the philosophical culture of our people. That such a book was possible, that it could be written, printed, sold, read, admired, believed by a people which claims a Kant, a Goethe, a Schopenhauer, is painful."

It is one of the curiosities of controversy that the Church should often be found defending with desperation, not her own positions, but some of the old, abandoned redoubts of Science. This was largely the case in the evolution controversy. The real "origin of species" was in the scientific mind. It was Science that discovered that all the multifarious forms of plant and animal life could be classified into distinct types, which, it too hastily assumed, were absolutely separate and fixed. When later Science came to revise that view, it discovered that the immutability of species had somehow in the meantime become a theological dogma, to be zealously defended by curates who could not tell a species from a genus.

It was the same in regard to the theory of spontaneous generation or the production of living beings from non-living matter. This was formerly good Christian doctrine, accepted by St. Augustine and taught by the medieval schoolmen, and when in 1674 the Italian physician, Francisco Redi, showed that the maggots that appeared in dead matter came from eggs, he was persecuted for unbelief. But it was still maintained that microscopic living forms could arise spontaneously in bouillon and infusions of hay until Pasteur proved that this was false, for in sealed and sterilized tubes no trace of life appears. Such negative experiments are, of course, not competent to prove that at some time and under other conditions life might not be produced from the non-living. Yet, strangely enough, Haeckel's theological opponents voluntarily adopted this untenable position and waged war against him especially on account of his belief that when the earth's crust cooled down, compounds of cyanic acid were transformed into globules of albumin, from which developed unicellular organisms.

The only alternative hypothesis to this which has been brought forward is the one advocated by Arrhenius, that the germs of life might have been brought from some other planet in meteorites or floating free in space and propelled by radiant energy. This is apparently not impossible, but it seems a very violent assumption, much harder of acceptance than the other, that of abiogenesis. For the wall between the organic and the inorganic has been broken down completely, and that between the living and non-living is being tunneled into from both sides. On the one hand we have been able to construct artificially such complex organic molecules as sugar and protein. On the other hand, it has been found possible to

[278]

produce in siliceous and metallic solutions mimic cells which grow, move, put forth pseudopodia, select their food, propagate by fission, and assume many of the characteristic forms of vegetable and animal life. In more than one laboratory experiments in the generation of life are still being hopefully carried on, and an announcement of their success at any time would not amaze biologists in general. But even though abiogenesis should forever remain impossible as a laboratory experiment, it would not be untenable as a hypothesis of the origin of life under the exceptional conditions of some earlier stage in the world's history. Such a supposition, whether true or not, is at least no more irreligious than is a recognition of the fact that non-living matter is being continuously transformed into living within our own bodies.

The volume invited attack because it was not only intentionally provocative, but unintentionally vulnerable. One does not have to be very learned in order to discover in it occasional errors as well as many extravagant and questionable statements. The fact that few people could treat of such a wide range of topics without making more mistakes than Haeckel did not, of course, protect him from criticism. Huxley, who enjoyed crossing swords with the clergy as much as Haeckel, was more careful to guard himself from counter attack.   If a discussion of demonology led unexpectedly to the question of the exact status of the district of Gadara in the Roman Empire, he was prepared to meet his opponents on that ground as well as in biology.   Not so Haeckel. He picks up his church history from infidel pamphleteers [1] and recklessly caricatures Christian beliefs. In attacking the dogma of the Immaculate Conception of Mary he confuses it with that of the Virgin Birth of Christ, and at the same time uses language needlessly offensive to those who regard the Mother of Jesus with adoration.[2]

A more serious charge than ignorance of ecclesiastical history was later brought against Haeckel by Doctor Brass, namely, that he had fabricated evidence in support of his theory of evolution by falsifying his drawings of embryos, that he had, among other things, taken away vertebræ from the tail of a monkey embryo and had extended the backbone of a human embryo in order to enhance the resemblance. Since accuracy is the soul of science, this is as serious

[1] President Thomas, of Middlebury College, exposed the source of his theory that the father of Christ was a Roman officer named Pandera in *The Independent*, Vol. 64, p. 515.

[2] Some of the more offensive of these passages are modified or eliminated in the later editions of "Die Weltratsel."

as it would be, for instance, to charge a minister with preaching miracles when he does not believe in them. In his reply Haeckel acknowledged

that a small part of my numerous embryo pictures (perhaps six or eight per cent) are actually "falsified" (in the sense of Doctor Brass), all those in fact in which the material at hand for observation was so incomplete or unsatisfactory that one was forced to fill up the gaps by hypothesis and to reconstruct the missing members by comparative synthesis in order to produce a connected chain of evolution.

Haeckel emphatically denies any deception or misrepresentation, and calls attention to the fact that such diagrammatic and reconstructed drawings are common to all physiological works and are necessary to bring out the desired points. As to whether Haeckel has transgressed the permissible limits of such schematization of material I should not be competent to decide. Thirty-six German men of science signed a condemnation of Haeckel; forty-seven German men of science, "though they did not like the kind of schematizing which Haeckel practiced in some cases", signed a condemnation of Brass and the Keplerbund. The numbers have no significance, since majorities never decide anything except the balance of opinion, but the group that stood by

Haeckel contained more embryologists and zoölogists than the other.

So I will dismiss the subject by quoting the opinion of a biologist and evolutionist who is thoroughly appreciative of Haeckel's contributions to science. Professor V. L. Kellogg, of Stanford University, in reviewing the "Evolution of Man" in *Science*, says :

"Biologists are likely to be of two minds concerning the advisability of putting Haeckel's 'Evolution of Man' into the hands of the lay reader as a guide and counselor on this most important of evolution subjects. Haeckel is such a proselytizer, such a scoffer and fighter of those who differ with him, that plain, unadorned statement of facts and description of things as they are cannot be looked for in his books. Or, if looked for, cannot be found. But this very eagerness to convince; this hoisting of a thesis, this fight for Haeckelian phylogeny and Haeckelian Monism, all make for interest and life in his writings."

This whole affair is a striking illustration of Huxley's observation that a controversy always shows an unfortunate tendency to slip from the question of what is right to the relatively unimportant question of who is right. Haeckel's critics have rarely attempted to controvert his scientific work and in fact would not in most cases be competent to discuss it. Even if he were guilty of all the mistakes alleged, it would not materially affect his scientific conclusions.

In noting Haeckel's faults, we are in danger of failing to appreciate the marvelous constructive genius of the man; the creative imagination which is characteristic of the great scientist even more than of the great poet. It was this gift that enabled him to discern in a handful of slime dredged up by the *Challenger* from the depths of the sea an orderly system of living beings wherein each microscopic skeleton of silica found its natural niche. It was this power which enabled him to assist so largely in the transformation of zoölogy from a purely observative and descriptive science, as it was when he began his labors, to a rational, experimental, and prophetic science, as it was when he closed them. As Cuvier from a few bits of bone could construct a whole animal, so Haeckel from scattered species ventured to construct, as early as 1865, a family tree, including all living forms from monera to man. Faulty it is from the standpoint of our present knowledge, but yet it must command our admiration because of the insight he showed in perceiving natural relationships and the skill with which he bridged the gaps in his living chain by hypothetical forms. Just as the great Russian chemist Mendeléef was able to describe in advance elements then unknown, but which were discovered later and found to fit into the vacant places he had assigned to them in his periodic law, so Haeckel's anticipations have been in many cases confirmed by later science. It was his good fortune to be able to hold in his hand the skullcap and femur of the "missing link" which had for years been the jest of the anti-evolutionists. The ape-man, or Pithecanthropus, which he had in 1885 described and named, was in 1894 discovered by Dubois in Java. The mind of Haeckel has such high tension that it leaps over the gaps in a demonstration like a ten thousand volt current.

His account of how he was led to doubt the dogma of the immutability of species must be quoted because it is an excellent illustration of the wisdom of the laboratory adage: "Study the exceptions. They prove some other rule."

The problem of the constancy or transmutation of species arrested me with a lively interest, when, twenty years ago, as a boy of twelve years, I made a resolute but fruitless effort to determine and distinguish the "good and bad species" of blackberries, willows, roses, and thistles. I look back now with fond satisfaction on the concern and painful skepticism that stirred my youthful spirits as I wavered and hesitated (in the manner of most "good classifiers", as we called them) whether to admit only "good" specimens into my herbarium and reject the "bad", or to embrace the latter and form a complete chain of transitional forms between the "good species" that would make an end of all their "goodness." I got out of the difficulty at the time by a compromise that I can recommend to all classifiers. I made two collections. One, arranged on official lines, offered to the sympathetic observer all the species, in "typical" specimens, as radically distinct forms, each decked with its pretty label; the other was a private collection, only shown to one trusted friend, and contained only the rejected kinds that Goethe so happily called "the characterless or disorderly races, which we hardly dare ascribe to a species, as they lose themselves in infinite varieties", such as rubus, salix, verbascum, hieracium, rosa, cirsium, etc. In this a large number of specimens, arranged in a long series, illustrated the direct transition from one good species to another. They were the officially forbidden fruit of knowledge, in which I took a secret boyish delight in my leisure hours. — Bölsche's "Life of Haeckel", p. 38.

Ernst Heinrich Philipp August Haeckel, to give him for once his full baptismal name, was born in Potsdam, February 16, 1834. He has a double inheritance of talent, for both the Haeckels and the Sethes, his mother's family, have contributed prominent names to German history, and the two families have intermarried more than once. It is a curious fact that Gustav Freytag, in his series of "Pictures from the German Past", should have chosen for his representative men of the nineteenth century two of Haeckel's ancestors : his mother's father, Christopher Sethe, Privy Councilor and defender of Prussia against Napoleon, and his father, Karl Haeckel, State Councilor.

But Ernst did not follow the family tradition and take to the law. He showed an unmistakable bent for natural science, so, as a compromise profession, his father had him trained as a physician. He took the medical course, and in obedience to his father's wishes consented to practice the profession for a year to see if he could make a success of it. During the year only three patients came to him, owing perhaps to the fact that Haeckel in order to get time for his biological researches had fixed his consultation hours from five to six in the morning. His father then gave up trying to make a doctor out of him and allowed him to go to Messina in 1859 to study marine animals. Haeckel straightway became engaged to his cousin Anna Sethe, and as soon as he got his appointment at Jena married her. Their happiness was brief. Two years later she died, leaving Haeckel, then thirty, so stricken that he felt that he could not long survive the blow, so he plunged with feverish haste into the preparation of his "General Morphology" in order to leave to the world his science and philosophy in a systematic form. It was written and printed, two thick volumes of more than twelve hundred pages, in less than a year, during which Haeckel lived like a hermit, working all day long and half the night, getting barely three or four hours sleep out of the twenty-four.

Haeckel immortalized his wife by giving her a living monument instead of one of marble or brass. He named for her one of his beloved medusæ, a fairy-like jellyfish, whose mass of long, trailing tentacles reminded him of his wife's blond hair. The Mitrocoma Annæ is described in his "Monograph on the Medusæ", published in 1864, and a note states that it was so named [1]

in memory of my dear, never-to-be-forgotten wife, Anna Sethe. If it is given to me to do something during my earthly pilgrimage for science and humanity, I owe it for the most part to the blessed influence of my gifted wife, who was torn from me by a premature end in 1864.

Three years afterwards he married again, Agnes

---

[1] Another medusa also named for his wife, Demomema Annasethe, will be found on one of the color plates of the New International Encyclopedia (Vol. XII, p. 68).

Huschke, daughter of a Jena anatomist. They have three children, two daughters and a son, who has inherited his father's artistic talent and has devoted himself to art in Munich.

Haeckel's æsthetic taste is shown not merely in the thousands of paintings and drawings that fill his monographs, but especially in his "Art Forms of Nature", which consists of ten portfolios of large color plates depicting strange and beautiful creatures from all realms of animal life but particularly in little known lower forms, fishes, crustaceans, corals, radiolaria, diatoms, and desmids. Here are to be seen real gargoyles, more grotesque than a sculptor's unaided imagination can create. Here the designer and decorator can find hundreds of suggestive themes for almost any purpose, so they have no excuse for repeating the trite and traditional forms as they do.

A large part of these "art forms" Haeckel discovered in the course of his investigations of deep-sea life on the material gathered by the *Challenger*, which was commissioned by the British Government in 1872–1875 to explore the ocean. The results of this expedition, published in fifty large volumes, constituted the greatest contribution to oceanography that has ever been made. Haeckel contributed the volumes on the medusæ, the siphonophora, the keratosa, and the radiolaria. To the radiolaria Haeckel devoted ten years, 1877–1887, and described 4318 species and 739 genera, from the curiously complicated siliceous skeletons deposited on the bottom of the ocean by these minute one-celled creatures.

Although Haeckel's life was largely devoted to the closest study of the minutest forms of life, yet he never lost sight of the broader aspects of his science. It seems as though he felt the need of resting his eyes by raising them from the microscope and looking out of the window to focus on infinity. Haeckel is essentially a specialist with a fondness for generalization. He welcomed the change in the current of thought that set in at the close of the nineteenth century, the effort of the new century to get at the inner meaning of the mass of miscellaneous facts that the old century had heaped up. It was with intent to assist in this movement that he produced, at the age of sixty-five, his "Riddle of the Universe", intending this to be the final expression of his view of the world, a fragmentary sketch instead of the complete "System of Monistic Philosophy" which he had projected many years ago and could not now hope to complete. But five years later he supplemented this with a similar popular volume, "The

Wonders of Life", in which he replies to certain criticisms and explains the biological principles on which his philosophy is based. This, unlike the "Riddle", was not composed at various intervals in the course of many years, but was written uninterruptedly during four months spent at Rapallo, on the Italian Riviera, when he was

> stimulated by the constant sight of the blue Mediterranean, the countless inhabitants of which had, for fifty years, afforded such ample material for my biological studies; and my solitary walks in the wild gorges of the Ligurian Apennines and the moving spectacle of its forest-crowned altars, inspired me with a feeling of the unity of living nature — a feeling that only too easily fades away in the study of detail in the laboratory.

Professor Haeckel retired from active service as teacher and investigator in 1909 at the age of seventy-five. "Indeed I am wholly a child of the nineteenth century and with its close I draw the line under my life's work," he said, and the publication of "The Wonders of Life" in 1904 confirms rather than contradicts this, for it shows that he maintains his position altogether unshaken by the revolution that has taken place in philosophic thought. Like Herbert Spencer he lived to see a reaction against many of the opinions for which he fought most earnestly.

ERNST HAECKEL

The nineteenth century was cocksure of so many things about which the twentieth century doubts. We are not so certain that, as Haeckel says, everything can be reduced to the motion of the atoms. The atom itself is crumbling, and as for motion, what is it? The ether in the reality of which Haeckel puts implicit faith is to us a doubtful, perhaps an unnecessary, hypothesis. Vitalism and teleology are coming back again into biology in new forms. Pluralism, not monism, is the fashion of the day, and some carry it almost to polytheism. Indeterminism finds more advocates nowadays than determinism. Haeckel makes the first law of thermodynamics (conservation of energy) one of the corner stones of his philosophy, but has little regard for the second (degradation of energy). Modern thought considers the second law more important than the first.[1]

And what shall we say about the "Law of Substance", which is Haeckel's contribution to the fundamental principles and which he apparently regards as of equal importance to the discoveries of Lavoisier and Mayer?[2] Speaking for myself, the reason I

[1] The significance of this change of emphasis in its bearing on metaphysical, religious, and ethical ideas I endeavored to explain in the preceding chapter.

[2] See Number 20 of the thirty theses given above.

[291]

cannot accept it is because it is absolutely meaningless to me. We know what the law of the conservation of matter means. It means, among other things, that 12 pounds of carbon when burned make 44 pounds of carbon dioxid, which we may decompose and get back 12 pounds of carbon again. The law of the conservation of energy means, among other things, that when we burn 12 pounds of carbon we produce 135,305,600 foot pounds of energy. But what does it mean when we say that matter and energy, or body and spirit, are somehow the same substance? Have we said more than when we affirmed the two laws separately? Even if true, does it make a bit of difference to anybody or anything; or to put the query into the pragmatic form, can it be true if it does not make a bit of difference to anybody or anything? But we must bear in mind that the rigid application of this formula to many historic attempts to solve the "riddle of the universe" would leave less of them intact than in the case of Haeckel.

The Christian reader is likely, in his irritation at what appears to him to be willful misrepresentation of his beliefs, to be too sweeping in his condemnation of the ideas of Haeckel. Even in the matter of religion Haeckel is not nearly so heretical as he assumes or is presumed to be. Many of the things he attacks are almost unrecognizable caricatures of modern religious views. It should be remembered that the "Riddle" and the "Wonders" were written at a time when he saw the German Government coming under the domination of the Blue-Black Block, and when it seemed to him that this coalition of conservatives and clericals threatened to suppress free speech and to check the advance of science. In his earlier writings his views are expressed in much more conciliatory language. Indeed, his pantheism is hardly distinguishable at times from theories of divine immanence such as are now held very commonly in orthodox churches. Wherein lies the magic of the word "Monism" if not in our ingrained prejudice in favor of unity, inherited from the fierce monotheism of the Jews? Is not Haeckel then borrowing the thunders of Sinai to enforce his new religion?

His "General Morphology" of 1866, which, as he told me, he prefers to his later works as an expression of his philosophy, concludes with the following passage:

Our philosophy knows only one God, and this Almighty God dominates the whole of nature without exception. We see his activity in all phenomena without exception. The whole of the inorganic world is subject to him just as much as the organic. If a body falls fifteen feet in the first second in empty space, if three atoms of oxygen unite with one atom of sulphur to form sulphuric acid, if the angle that is formed by the contiguous surfaces of a column of rock-crystal is always 120°, these phenomena are just as truly the direct action of God as the flowering of the plant, the movement of the animal, or the thought of man. We all exist "by the grace of God", the stone as well as the water, the radiolarian as well as the pine, the gorilla as well as the Emperor of China. No other conception of God except this that sees his spirit and force in all natural phenomena is worthy of his all-enfolding greatness; only when we trace all forces and all movements, all the forms and properties of matter, to God, as the sustainer of all things, do we reach the human idea and reverence for him that really corresponds to his infinite greatness. In him we live, and move, and have our being. Thus does natural philosophy become a theology. The cult of nature passes into that service of God of which Goethe says: "Assuredly there is no nobler reverence for God than that which springs up in our heart for conversation with nature." God is almighty: he is the sole sustainer and cause of all things. In other words, God is the universal law of causality. God is absolutely perfect; he cannot act in any other than a perfectly good manner; he cannot therefore act arbitrarily or freely — God is necessity. God is the sum of all force, and therefore of all matter. Every conception of God that separates him from matter, and opposes to him a sum of forces that are not of a divine nature, leads to amphitheism (or ditheism) and on to polytheism. In showing the unity of the whole of nature, Monism points out that only one God exists, and that this God reveals himself in all the phenomena of nature. In grounding all the phenomena of organic or inorganic nature on the universal law of causality, and exhibiting them as the outcome of "efficient causes", Monism proves that God is the necessary cause of all things and the law itself. In recognizing none but divine forces in nature, in proclaiming all natural laws to be divine, Monism rises to the greatest and most lofty conception of which man, the most perfect of all things, is capable, the conception of the unity of God and nature.

How to Read Haeckel

"The Riddle of the Universe" (Harper) is the best popular presentation of science and philosophy from Haeckel's point of view. This may be supplemented by "The Wonders of Life" (Harper), in which he develops more fully the biological side and defends himself against certain criticisms. To these should be added the very interesting life of Haeckel by W. Bölsche (Jacobs). Cheap editions of these three are published by the Rationalist Press Association, London. They, as well as other works of Haeckel, are translated by Joseph McCabe.

"The Natural History of Creation" (Appleton) and "The Evolution of Man" (Appleton or Putnam) are both intended to explain in a way comprehensible to the general reader the fundamental principles of the theory of evolution and the biological facts on which it is based. Special addresses by Haeckel are translated under the titles of: "Monism as Connecting Religion and Science" (Macmillan) and "Last Words on Evolution" (New York). Of his "Indische Reisebilder" there are two versions in English; one by Mrs. S. E. Boggs entitled "India and Ceylon", which is neither literal nor complete, and one by Clara Bell, "A Visit to Ceylon" (Eckler), which is better. On the personal side may be read Herman Schauffauer's sketches, "Haeckel, a Colossus of Science" (*North American Review*, August, 1910), and "A Talk with Haeckel at Home", in *T. P.'s Magazine*, 1912; Elbert Hubbard's "Little Journeys to the Homes of Great Scientists", and Joseph McCabe's "A Scientist's Sunset Years", in *Harper's Weekly*, August 7, 1909. A few of the more noteworthy of the books and articles on Haeckelism in English are: "Life and Matter", by Sir Oliver Lodge, a criticism from the standpoint of a spiritualist; the discussion between Lodge and McCabe in *Hibbert Journal*, Vol. III, pp. 315 and 741; "The World View of a Scientist", by Frank Thilly in *Popular Science Monthly*, Vol. LXI, pp. 407–425; "Ernst Haeckel, Darwinist, Monist", by V. L. Kellogg, in *Popular Science Monthly*, Vol. LXXVI, pp. 136–142; "Haeckel and Monism", by J. Butler Burke, in *Oxford and Cambridge Review*, 1907; "Lucretius and Haeckel", by F. B. R. Hellems, in "University of Colorado Studies", Vol. III, 1905; "Religion as a Credible Doctrine", by W. H. Mallock; "Haeckel's Monism False", by Reverend F. Ballard; "The Old Riddle and the Newest Answer", by Father Gerard; "Haeckel's Critics Answered", by Joseph McCabe (London: Rationalist Press); "Haeckel's Answer to the Jesuits" (New York: *Truthseeker*); "Haeckel and His Methods", by R. L. Mangan, in the *Catholic World*, May, 1909. The monism of Doctor Paul

ERNST HAECKEL

Carus, of Chicago, is a different variety from Haeckel's as he has pointed out in the *Monist*, Vol. II, p. 498; Vol. IV, p. 228; and Vol. XVI, p. 120.

Of the immense body of literature in German on Haeckel it is impossible to give more than a few selected titles. The bibliography appended to "Ernst Haeckel: Versuch einer Chronik seines Lebens und Wirkens" by Walther May (Leipzig: Barth, 1909) devotes fourteen pages to the titles of Haeckel's writings, four pages to a list of biographical books and sketches, and thirteen pages to a list of criticisms and discussions of Haeckelism.

"Die Welträtsel" and "Die Lebenswunder" are published by Alfred Kröner, Leipzig. The epitome of Haeckel's philosophy, which is given almost entire in the preceding pages, is to be found in "Der Monistenbund", *Thesen zur Organisation des Monismus* (Neuer Frankfurter Verlag). Other works of Haeckel of a general and philosophical character are: "Natürliche Schöpfungs-Geschichte" (Berlin: Reimer); "Anthropogenie oder Entwickelungsgeschichte des Menschens" (Leipzig: Engelmann); "Generalle Morphologie der Organismen" (Reimer); "Systematische Phylogenie" (Reimer); "Der Kampf um den Entwickelungs-Gedanken" (Reimer); "Der Monismus als Band zwischen Religion und Wissenschaft" (Kröner); "Freie Wissenschaft und freie Lehre", the reply to Virchow (Kröner); "Das Weltbild von Darwin und Lamarck", the centenary address on Darwin's birthday (Kröner).

Haeckel's travel sketches are to be found in "Inisdiche Reisebriefe" (Berlin: Paetel) and "Aus Insulinde" (Kröner). Even one who reads no German will find enjoyment and gain an appreciation of the artistic side of Haeckel by looking over the color plates in "Kunstformen der Natur" (Leipzig: Bibliographisches Institut) or "Wanderbilder" (Gera: Köhler).

A remarkable tribute of world-wide affection is the volume issued on his eightieth birthday, "Was wir Ernst Haeckel verdanken" (Leipzig: Verlag Unesma), to which one hundred and twenty-five men and women contributed, — savants, artists, workingmen, officials, and businessmen.

The monistic movement may be followed by the pamphlets of the society which may be obtained ordinarily from the Verlag Unesma, Leipzig. Some of the more interesting of these *Flugschriften* are: "Friedrich Paulsen über Ernst Haeckel", by Albrecht Rau; "Reinke contra Haeckel", by Heinrich Schmidt; "Eine neue Reformation vom Christentum zum Monismus", by Hannah Dorsch and Arnold Dodel; "Monismus und Christentum", by Heinrich Schmidt; "Monismus und Klerikalismus", by J. Unold; "Das Einheit der physikochemischen Wissenschaften", by Wilhelm Ostwald; "Die einheitliche Weltanschauung", by Ernst Diesing: this last urges the Monists to support the peace and conservation movements. The official organ is *Das monistische Jahrhundert,* a weekly edited by Ostwald and published by the Verlag Unesma, Leipzig. The issue for February 14, 1914, is, in honor of his eightieth birthday, devoted to Haeckel. For the history of monistic philosophy in general from the Greeks to the present time see "Der Monismus", by various authors, under the editorship of Arthur Drews (Jena: Diederich, 1908) or "Geschichte des Monismus", by Rudolf Eisler (Leipzig: Kröner).

Of the expository and controversial literature, pro

and con, it must suffice to mention the following titles: "Die Weltanschauung Haeckel", by Max Upel (Berlin-Schoenberg; Buchverlag der Hilfe), a brief and fairminded critique; "Ernst Haeckel, ein Bild seines Lebens und seiner Arbeit", by Wilhelm Breitenbach (Brackwede i. W.: Verlag von Breitenbach & Hoerster), a tribute to the master on his seventieth birthday; "Haeckel's Welträthsel nach ihren starken und ihren schwachen Seite", by Julius Baumann (Leipzig: Diederich, 1900); "Anti-Haeckel", by F. Loofs, Professor of Theology in Halle; "Philosophia Militans" by F. Paulsen, Professor of Philosophy in Berlin. A good account of the Haeckel-Paulsen controversy by Theodor Lorenz may be found in *Deutsche Literaturzeitung*, March 12, 1910, and later.